British Lorries
1900-1992

Above:
**This Morris design of 10cwt van and truck
proved popular with small concerns when
introduced in 1938. The engine was offset to
give room for the driver's legs.**

Overleaf:
**Two 1961 'Sputnik' cab Foden S21 eight-wheel
tankers in the fleet of Monsanto Chemicals.
They were used to carry chemicals to plastics,
paint and paper manufacturers throughout
most of Britain, the Netherlands and Germany.**

THE
IAN ALLAN
TRANSPORT
LIBRARY

Ian Allan
Publishing

British Lorries

1900-1992

S.W. Stevens-Stratten

First published 1992
Reprinted 1993, 1994
This impression 1995

ISBN 0 7110 2091 4

Published by Ian Allan Ltd, Shepperton, Surrey;
and printed in Great Britain by
Ian Allan Printing Ltd Coombelands House,
Addlestone, Surrey KT15 1HY.

Contents

Part 1

Some Smaller British Manufacturers

Left:
A Pagefield mobile crane, similar to the ones used by the railway companies, loading a container on to a Pagefield lorry chassis, c1929.

Part 2

Right:
An ERF turbo-charged diesel CP series pictured in 1984.

Front cover:
A 1969 Atkinson Raider which was rebuilt and re-registered in 1978. Fitted with a Gardner 180 engine it is still in revenue earning service. Seen at the Sandwell Rally in May 1992. *P. Durham*

Back cover, top:
Two preserved stalwarts. On the left is a 1958 AEC Mammoth Six, and on the right is a 1948 Leyland Beaver 7½ ton lorry. Both are now owned by Mr R. Rainey of Yeovil. *P. Durham*

Back cover, bottom:
A 1948 ERF model C15 with Gardner 5LW engine and a David Brown gearbox, seen at the Midland Festival of Transport, Weston Park in April 1992. *P. Durham*

British Lorries
1900–1945

Introduction

'Natural progression' are two words widely used today to describe many different spheres of development, but in the field of mechanised transport the changes made in this century have had a significant effect on the lives of men and women in the greater part of the world. It is not only the motor car which has caused such dramatic changes to our lifestyle, but the progress and development made in buses and coaches, lorries and vans; even the farm tractor, for they have all played their part.

The transformation from the early days of commercial vehicles to the present time, despite restrictions and government legislation, are quite remarkable and the last 70 years have seen more changes than in most other forms of transport — not only the aesthetic or visual impact, but in terms of technical development.

Today a heavy lorry can undertake the journey from London to Bristol in 2½hr, carrying a load of 32tons reliably and safely, with the driver sitting in comfort protected from the weather, with heater, radio and cassette player in his cab. Such a journey 70 years ago would take as many days as it now takes hours, breakdowns were numerous, average speed was less than 12mph, with the driver exposed to all the elements, sitting on a wooden plank, with virtually no springing or suspension on the vehicle and with poor road surfaces, a rough ride was inevitable. Incidentally, the load carried was unlikely to have exceeded 4/5tons. One must not forget the horse, a noble and intelligent animal, but a story beyond the scope of this book.

The earlier book, compiled by my colleague and friend, the late Charles F. Klapper, was originally my idea. In compiling this present volume I have tried to portray a general selection of the vehicles seen on the road for the given period, but obviously it is not possible to mention or illustrate all the models produced, so I have tried to show some of the more popular vehicles, plus a few unusual ones. Naturally, the book confines itself to goods vehicles and is not intended to include examples of lorries which are bus-derived, or strange 'one-off' or specialised items.

Below:
A 1938 Foden tractor produced in 1938 for a fairground operator which is still in use in the 1980s. *S. W. Stevens-Stratten*

I purposely have not included the small band of foreign makers who imported a few of their vehicles to this country and only partly assembled or serviced them here, for that is a subject in itself.

Unfortunately, many of the manufacturers' featured in this book are no longer in business. In fact of the 48 makers mentioned, only nine are still in existence, and of this nine only two are still wholly British owned.

A few of the smaller British producers of commercial vehicles are included in the last chapter.

The text concerning each manufacturer is not intended to be a complete history, but more to give the salient points regarding the development of the company and its production.

I have tried to show vehicles which are actually in working trim, rather than manufacturers preproduction photographs, which are often misleading. Some photographs of preserved vehicles have been included because the original is not available or has been seen in other publications.

Thanks must be given to the enthusiasts who have lovingly restored some of the old vehicles, spending a considerable amount of their time and money to give enjoyment to others. The Historic Commercial Vehicle Society (HCVS) was formed in 1956 to cater for the growing band of enthusiasts and is now the leading organisation in this field. There are many museums up and down the country where preserved vehicles are exhibited, and it would not be practical to list them all here, but mention must be made of the National Motor Museum at Beaulieu, Hampshire, and the British Commercial Vehicle Museum at Leyland, Lancashire. Both are well worth a visit.

I hope that this book will not only be useful as a work of reference for enthusiasts interested in old commercials, but it will also be a trip down memory lane for some of the older readers.

S. W. Stevens-Stratten FRSA
Epsom, Surrey

All photographs are from the Ian Allan Library unless otherwise credited

AEC

The Associated Equipment Company (AEC) had its origins in Walthamstow as the servicing concern for the London Motor Omnibus Company (fleet name Vanguard), in 1906. A few years later Vanguard joined with others to form the London General Omnibus Co. This association with the old Vanguard firm was maintained as the telegraphic address for AEC remained 'Vangastow' until the end of its days.

On 13 June 1902, AEC was formed as a separate entity to build buses for London with the X-type and later the famous B-type coming into service. The first commercial vehicle was actually a lorry on the X-type chassis, but not until World War 1 did AEC come into commercial vehicle production in earnest with a contract for 3ton army lorries, designated the Y-type, of which more than 10,000 were built on a production line from 1916 to the end of the hostilities.

Variations on the Y-type were produced for the civilian market until 1923 when a 2½ton chassis was introduced. This was the smallest vehicle AEC ever produced, all others having a minimum payload of 6tons, but this model developed into the 204-type which remained in production until 1928.

The financial situation in the country was at a low ebb in 1926 and AEC entered into an agreement with Daimler for joint marketing under the name Associated Daimler. This only lasted for two years, after which both companies resumed their independent existence.

The fortunes of AEC rose rapidly and a brand new factory was built at Southall, with the move from Walthamstow completed in 1927. Another milestone was the appointment of G. J. Rackham as Chief Engineer and Designer in 1928 for his new ideas were incorporated in the production and the name of AEC became synonymous with quality and reliability.

From 1930 new models appeared with the now famous AEC inverted triangular badge, the range consisting of named models, all beginning with the letter M — Mammoth, Mercury, Majestic, etc. These models proved so successful that with a few exceptions they remained in production, with minor updated modifications until the end of World War 2. AEC was also in the forefront of the production of the diesel engine, offering this as an alternative to the petrol engine in the mid-1930s.

During World War 2, the company had an impressive record with the manufacture of Matador and Marshal vehicles for the services, as well as tanks and special components, also undertaking many experimental projects on behalf of the government.

Below:
In 1916 the standard Y type subsidy 3ton lorry was introduced and a year later an improved model, the YA type, was made. Over 10,000 of these vehicles were supplied to the War Department by 1919. A 30hp engine was fitted. Many of these vehicles were purchased by civilian operators after the war, and the basically similar YB and YC types continued in production until 1921.

Top:
Still on solid tyres in 1930, although by this time pneumatics could be fitted, this Mammoth 7/8ton lorry had a six-cylinder overhead valve engine developing 110bhp (45hp on RAC rating) with a wheelbase of 16ft 7in.

Above:
A normal control Mercury canvas covered truck of 1928-29, for 4ton payloads. The wheelbase is 14ft and overall length 21ft 7in. The petrol tank was under the driver's seat.

Top:
One of 10 Mercury (model 640) 3½ton tankers which were supplied in 1930 to the Anglo American Oil Co. A four-cylinder petrol engine developed 65bhp at 2,000rpm. The wheelbase was 14ft and the total length was 20ft 5in.

Above:
The Matador 5ton chassis was introduced in 1932, and had many similarities with the Mercury, but this particular vehicle was fitted with an AEC/Ricardo oil engine.

Above:
The normal control Majestic of 1930 (model 666) was for 6ton payloads and from 1931 was only available on pneumatic tyres, but there was the option of a petrol or diesel engine.

Centre left:
The Monarch Mk II (model 637) of 1933 was an updated version of the original type of the same name introduced three years earlier as model 641. The payload was increased to 7½ton and alternative petrol or oil engines were offered. This model remained in production until 1935.

Bottom left:
This 1934 Mammoth Major eight-wheeled tank lorry was purchased new by a Liverpool concern and is now preserved by the Science Museum. The Mammoth Major Mk II was introduced in 1935 for 15ton loads and remained in production until 1948, when the Mk III appeared, although it was basically similar.
S. W. Stevens-Stratten

13

Albion

The Albion Motor Company was founded by T. Blackwood-Murray and N. O. Fulton (late of Arrol-Johnson), at Bathgate in Scotland in 1901. In that year it manufactured a tiller-steered, two-cylinder, 8hp dogcart. A year later the firm put a van body to a somewhat similar vehicle to carry 10cwt loads (later the engine size was increased to 10hp). This was the beginning of a highly successful company, for in 1904 Albion moved to a large factory at Scotstoun.

Many different models were made in their first decade, the most successful being the A10 model which appeared in 1910 for 3/4ton loads using a four-cylinder, 32hp engine. Like most Albions, the success lay in the simplicity of the original design, for example a patented ignition system devised by W. Blackwood-Murray, which continued from the early days until 1923. The A10 model made Albion well known for its reliability and it lasted in

Below:
A 1907 model A3 15cwt van with a 16hp engine. This model was in production from 1904 to 1915.

production for 16 years, and by the end of the war in 1918, nearly 6,000 had been supplied to the services.

In the 1920s Albion adopted the slogan 'Sure as the Sunrise' and the radiators had the setting sun motif with the name Albion in the distinctive lettering. During the 1920s and 1930s the firm prospered and many new models were introduced ranging from 30cwt to 15ton. Albion was early in the field with the forward control layout, which it called 'cab-over' types. Apart from its bus chassis, Albion was late in giving names to its range of vehicles, and used an unwieldy combination of letters and figures to denote the chassis model.

In 1935 Albion acquired the factory used to produce the Halley vehicles, which had ceased manufacture, and the building was used as a service depot, also as a packing plant for spares and export CKD vehicles.

Albion also made the chassis for a number of Merryweather fire appliances, most of which were fitted with Albion engines.

In World War 2, Albion made many vehicles for the services including some large tractive units for tank transporters and recovery work.

Above:
The longest production record is for the model T Ford, but this surely must come second. The Albion model A10 3ton chassis was made from 1910-1926. Powered by a four-cylinder 32hp engine, it had a wheelbase of 13ft 1in, but in 1920 it was available with an extended wheelbase of 14ft 5in.

Below:
A 2½ton platform lorry of 1932. The shape of the cab is typical of many vehicles of the 1920s.

Above right:
Albion was in the forefront for the forward control (or cab-over-engine) configuration, and this 5ton overtype van from 1931 is a typical example. It was owned by a well known firm of transport contractors.

Centre right:
A 3ton long-wheelbase, 14ft platform lorry. It was one of two used to carry casks of tobacco leaf from a bonded warehouse to a factory four miles away.

Below:
In 1936 Albion produced a popular chassis, designated B119, which was fitted with a four-cylinder petrol engine of 19.6hp. The wheelbase was 9ft 9in, and this example had a Strachans-built body with internal measurements of 13ft 6in length by 6ft 3in height.

Above:
Albion chassis were popular for the exotic coachwork of the decade. This 1935 example on a 30/40cwt chassis is by Holland Coachcraft, a firm which made similar bodies for Collars Ltd.

Below:
A 10ton six-wheeler fitted with an Albion six-cylinder direct injection oil engine. It was supplied to a Perth haulage contractor at the beginning of World War 2. It has an unladen weight of 5ton 12cwt.

Armstrong-Saurer

Saurer vehicles were produced in Switzerland and had an enviable reputation for their strength and reliability. As far back as 1907 Pickfords had imported a number, and ordered more in the 1920s. In 1930 the Saurer organisation decided that its vehicles should be made in the UK under licence, and thus Armstrong Whitworth began the manufacture at its Scotswood-on-Tyne works. The first Armstrong-Saurer, as the English models were named, was shown at the Commercial Motor Show in 1931. Originally it had been intended that all the complete vehicles would be built on Tyneside, but with production also taking place near Paris, some parts were imported — a similar practice being perfected by Ford some four decades later.

The Armstrong-Saurer vehicles proved successful and popular with all who were engaged in the heavy haulage business, and when eventually replaced, many ended their days with fairground operators. The vehicles had a rugged look about them, which indeed was indicative of the whole breed. Saurer was an early champion of the oil engine, with which its lorries were all fitted, also air-brakes and overdrive — great advances for the early 1930s.

All the models were given names such as the Active, 7ton rigid four-wheeler; the Dynamic, 9 and 10ton six-wheeler, the Samson, 15ton rigid eight, etc. Production ceased in 1937, and unfortunately, as far as we know, only one has been preserved.

Below:
The Durable 6/7ton chassis was supplied with the six-cylinder 110bhp oil engine. This vehicle with an insulated van body for the carriage of meat was the fifth repeat order from Fairclough Bros in 1933.

Right:
A 7ton Dominant six-wheeler in use by a firm known for road surfaces. The Dominant remained in production from 1932-34 and the price of the chassis was £1,750.

Below right:
The Effective 6/7tonner (12/14tons with trailer) was produced from 1934 until manufacture ceased. It was also fitted with the six-cylinder 110bhp engine of 111mm bore by 150mm stroke.

Atkinson

The name of Atkinson, in the field of road transport, goes back to 1907, when Edward Atkinson began to service and repair steam wagons and became an agent for Alley & McLellan, the originators of the Sentinel steamcars.

The first steam wagon to carry the Atkinson name was built in 1916, a conventional four-wheeler for a 6ton payload, and production reached three vehicles a week in the early 1920s.

Despite its production of steamers, the firm floundered financially in the depression of the late 1920s, but continued to undertake the construction of trailers and the servicing and repair of vehicles.

The company was reconstituted as Atkinson Lorries Ltd in 1933 under the management of W. G. Allen of Nightingale Garage of Clapham (South London). A conventional forward control 6ton four-wheel vehicle was produced using the Gardner diesel engine as the power unit. This was followed by a six-wheeler using the same cab and in 1937 an eight-wheeled rigid for 15ton payloads. From then on the company never looked back and although producing only a few vehicles they were of high quality and began to win favourable comments from their operators.

Wartime contracts enhanced Atkinson's position, particularly on the financial side, for in 1940 it was awarded a Ministry of Supply contract for 60 six-wheel chassis fitted with Gardner 6LW engines, followed a year later by an order for 100 similar chassis, but this time fitted with the AEC 7.7 litre engine, and finally another 100 similarly engined chassis.

After World War 2, Atkinson launched a new range of four-, six- and eight-wheeled vehicles, all employing Gardner engines.

Below:
This Atkinson Colonial steam lorry was built in 1918. It is believed to be the only one in preservation and was brought back from Australia. The three-way tipping body carries a 6ton load.

Right:
A 9½/10ton 'Chinese' six-wheeler which was produced in 1937. The cab is standard for all Atkinson models of this era.

Below right:
An eight-wheeled 15tonner of 1938 engaged on night trunk routes.

Austin

The name Austin is usually associated with cars and the Austin Seven or 'Chummy' in particular. The first cars were produced in 1908 and shortly afterwards a van body was fitted to one of these early models. The first real commercial vehicle was a 3ton lorry produced in 1913, and this was perhaps unique as it had a forward control layout — the engine being on and slightly below the cab floor, with the radiator behind the four-cylinder 29hp engine. There was also divided drive, two prop shafts each driving a bevel connected to the stub rear axles.

The production of commercial vehicles never achieved prominence and finished in 1922; the years following only seeing light vans based on car chassis with similar engines. Ambulances were also car-derived and based on the Austin 18 or 20 saloon models.

The company seriously entered the commercial vehicle market again in 1938 when it developed a range of lorries and vans ranging from 30cwt to 5ton. Outwardly the range resembled their rivals Bedford, the difference being noticeable in the radiator — in fact the new range became known as the Birmingham Bedfords.

During World War 2, Austin made many vehicles for the services, including the 2/3ton K2 chassis for army ambulances and the ATVs (auxiliary towing vehicles) for the fire services; the K3 general service 3tonner; the K5 four-wheel drive 3tonners (known as 'Screamers' due to the noise from the gearbox and transmission); and the K6 and 6×4-type used as RAF bowsers (aircraft refuellers).

Below:
An Austin 10/12cwt van which is based on the Austin Twenty car chassis. This type of vehicle was built from 1924 onwards. From the end of 1929 two wheelbases were offered — 10ft 10in or 11ft 4in — and in 1932 synchromesh gearboxes were introduced.

Right:
One of the many ambulances which were built on the Austin Twenty chassis. This example dates from 1936.

Below right:
Again using a car chassis, this is the 1937 version of the 12hp van.

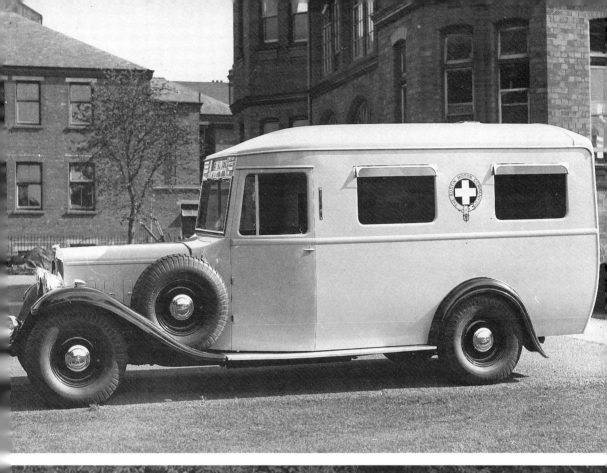

Below:
The immediate prewar Austin 5ton chassis showing the rear of the cab and inside of the wooden planked lorry.

DER 219

Left:
The handsome lines of the radiator, bonnet and cab of the K series of commercial vehicles which appeared in 1939. This is a well restored K2 truck, a 2/3tonner using a six-cylinder petrol engine of 26.8hp. Lockheed hydraulic brakes operated on all wheels. *S. W. Stevens-Stratten*

Top:
The Austin 5ton chassis carrying a petrol tank body.

Above:
Again, pleasing lines for the design of this 30cwt box van supplied to Liverpool Corporation for distributing milk to hospitals in the area.

25

Bean

Bean Cars Ltd, with its works at Waddams Pool, Tipton, Dudley, Worcestershire, was an offshoot of A. Harper & Sons Ltd which was founded in 1901 and was well established as a component manufacturer for the motor vehicle industry. In 1919 the company decided to produce complete motor cars itself, and a few years later made its first commercial vehicle.

In 1925, Bean produced a 25cwt lorry with a 13.9hp engine selling at a competitive price and this was replaced two years later by an updated version. However, at this time the company had run into financial difficulties and the steel suppliers, Hadfield, had taken control of the company, although allowing Bean to keep its separate identity.

The 'Empire' chassis for 50cwt loads was produced and then in 1929 a 30cwt vehicle, using a 46bhp Hadfield engine from one of the Bean car range was offered for only £325. Bean decided that due to fierce competition in the car market it would concentrate solely on commercial vehicle

production, and in 1931 produced the New Era 20-25cwt chassis.

Competition in this market was equally fierce and Bean reduced the price of its products over the years in an effort to beat the larger firms such as Ford, Morris and Dodge, but in the end the profit margin became negligible and the company went into liquidation in 1931. Fortunately, the company was reformed and continued to supply components to the motor industry.

Below:
A 4ton forward control flat platform lorry of 1930.

Right:
In 1931 Bean introduced the 20/25cwt New Era chassis seen here as a delivery van.

Below right:
A fleet of New Era vans supplied to the Kensington catering firm of Slaters in 1931.

Beardmore

William Beardmore & Co Ltd are better known as the manufacturer of the taxicabs which it first produced in 1919, and these were so successful that the company carried out some market research and in 1923 brought out an improved model which, again, was highly popular. The taxicabs were manufactured in Paisley, Scotland and retailed through Beardmore's own taxicab company in London.

In 1930 the company acquired the patents for the production of the French Chenard-Walcker tractor, which via the coupling allowed part of the trailer weight to be taken on the tractor which, of course, increased the adhesion. The vehicles were produced at Clapham in South London.

Beardmore produced the Anaconda, a 15ton multi-wheeler; the Python for 10/15ton loads; and the Cobra which was a 10ton tractor unit. All used Meadows engines.

In 1932, Beardmore sold this part of its business to a syndicate calling itself Multiwheelers, which became an independent company. The engines in the vehicles were usually AEC or Gardner from this time onwards. Multiwheelers ceased production in 1937.

Below:
A Beardmore Cobra 10ton articulated unit manufactured in 1931. The coupling between tractor and trailer can be clearly seen.

Right:
A recently restored Beardmore articulated unit in 1984. *S. W. Stevens-Stratten*

Bedford (and Chevrolet)

Chevrolet vehicles had been imported from the USA and were even assembled at Hendon in the late 1920s. The last of these models were the LQ and LT trucks for 30cwt payloads, both using a six-cylinder engine of 26.6hp, with a 'splash' lubrication system, and known as the 'cast iron wonder'. The firm moved to Luton, and as its parent company, General Motors, wished to improve the sales and expand the Chevrolet range, it was placed under the wing of General Motors' car producer, Vauxhall Motors.

In 1931 the range was completely redesigned and produced under the name Bedford. Success was immediate, for the range proved to be fast and reliable which won it popularity with all branches of the road haulage industry. The Bedford slogan 'You See Them Everywhere' was absolutely true.

Their first models used the same cab as the Chevrolet, but there the difference ended. The first model (the WHG) was a 2tonner (10ft 11in wheelbase), the WLG was a 2tonner (13ft 1in wheelbase), and the WS was for 30cwt loads and a wheelbase of 10ft 11in. All three used the Bedford

Below:
One of the first 2ton Bedfords of 1931 — note the preface 'British' on the bonnet side. This long wheelbase version, complete with dropside body cost £260!

six-cylinder 26.3hp petrol engine, and all remained in production until 1939 when the new range was announced. In 1934 the model BYC 12cwt van was introduced which proved to be the best light delivery van in its class. In the same year the WTL model for tippers made an appearance. All these vehicles had flat fronted radiators.

In 1939, Bedford announced a completely new range with attractive curved radiator grilles and more curved cab outlines. The K models were for 30-40cwt payloads, with standard wheelbase of 10ft, using a six-cylinder 27.3hp petrol engine. The designations were KZ for chassis only; KC for chassis and cab; KD for a dropside lorry and KV for a van.

The M series was for 2-3ton loads with 10ft or 11ft 11in wheelbase, the designations being as for the K series, except MST which was the shorter wheelbase model as a tipper.

The O series was for 3/4ton and 5ton loads, with two alternative wheelbases, but apart from chassis and cab the range was for lorries or tippers. The shorter wheelbase (9ft 3in) was also available as a prime mover for articulated vehicles.

During World War 2 Bedford made many different kinds of vehicles for the Services, a total of 250,000, among them the famous QL range of forward control four-wheel drive vehicles.

Above:
This breakdown truck complete with crane and searchlight was new in 1934 to the London County Council Motor Vehicle Repair Depot.

Below:
An early 2ton chassis was used by Curtis for mounting a three-horse box shown here unloading at a hunt meeting.

Above:

A 3ton short wheelbase chassis is used for this hydraulic end tipper with the pump driven directly from the gearbox take-off. It is powered by the six-cylinder overhead valve 27hp engine, which had a long production run. The body has a steel-lined floor and top-hinged tailboard. The price in 1937 was £327.

Below:

The good-looking design of this 30cwt delivery van is evident in this side view, as is the generous space for signwriting or advertising.

Top left:
The 30cwt van was very popular before World War 2, and this is an example on contract hire to Cadbury-Fry.

Centre left:
HM Queen Elizabeth, now the Queen Mother, inspects a convoy of wartime Bedford vans donated by the American Committee for Air Raid Relief.

Below:
A 5ton Bedford chassis is used for this 900gal Thompson tank body which transported sodium sulphate for the Crow Carrying Co in 1941.

Bristol

The Bristol Tramways & Carriage Co Ltd was a bus operator which manufactured its own passenger carrying vehicles from 1908. It was not unnatural that the firm should produce a few commercial vehicles, the first two being exhibited at the Royal Agricultural Show in Bristol in 1913. These were a brewers' dray and a dairy produce wagon.

Eighteen vehicles were supplied to the RNAS between July 1914 and January 1915. The next production was an experimental W type lorry in 1915, and postwar production was a development of this in 1920 which was designated as the 4ton model. A total of 649 of this type of chassis was produced, at least 132 being fitted with commercial bodywork, mainly tankers and lorries. Production of this type finished in 1931.

A 2ton forward control model was introduced in 1923 and a total of 267 was built, initially 73 were fitted with commercial bodywork mainly for petrol distribution.

In 1932 Bristol became part of the Thomas Tilling Group and all commercial production ceased in favour of passenger chassis.

The firm, renamed Bristol Commercial Vehicles re-entered the goods vehicle field in 1953, which is outside the period covered by this volume.

Below:
This 1920 Bristol dropside lorry was exhibited at the 1920 Commercial Motor Show and was used by Bristol Tramways from 1923-31 when it was sold to a showman who used it until the early 1950s. It has since been fully restored and is seen here at the Wheels of Yesterday Rally in Battersea Park in 1986. *S. W. Stevens-Stratten*

Caledon

Scottish Commercial Cars Ltd of Duke Street, Glasgow was a distributor for Commer vehicles, but in 1914 found that these vehicles were unavailable for the civilian market. Realising that its main activity would suffer, the company decided to set up its own manufacturing concern, using Dorman engines and Dux gearboxes (from France).

The first vehicle was produced in 1915 and a range of 3, 3½ and 4ton chassis followed. The vehicles were basic and suffered from back axle problems among other malfunctions. At the end of World War 1 some 380 had been built, of which 76 were supplied to the Ministry of Munitions, after having been rejected earlier.

After the war the firm, now named Caledon Motors, was to produce a range from 30cwt to 7ton, also manufacturing its own engines. Unfortunately the flood of cheap and good ex-WD lorries coming on the market decreased potential sales to such an extent that the firm ran into financial difficulties as early as 1922, but it struggled on until 1926, when it was acquired by Garretts.

Below:
A 1919 Caledon model E 4ton lorry, which remained in production until 1926. Powered by a four-cylinder (120mm by 140mm) petrol engine, the maximum speed was 12mph at 5mpg. The wheelbase was 14ft 3in.
S. W. Stevens-Stratten

Commer

Commercial Cars Ltd was formed in 1905 and the title immediately shortened to Commer. The early models were designated CC and featured the Lindley epicyclic preselector gearbox, the gear lever unusually mounted on the steering column. Even its early models ranged from 1ton to 6ton which was quite a heavy vehicle for those days, and they were exported to many countries including the USA.

During World War 1, Commer produced over 3,000 model RC 4ton lorries. Soon after hostilities ended there were so many ex-WD vehicles coming on the market that Commer, like other manufacturers, was not selling new vehicles and this, plus the general depression of the mid-1920s led the company into financial difficulties.

Commer was taken over by Humber Cars in 1926. Humber renamed its Centaur Co (founded in 1911) as Commer Cars Ltd. Hence the use of the name Centaur (and Raider) for some of the Commer range in the 1930s.

The Rootes Group took over the Humber/ Hillman/Commer companies in 1928, and from then onwards Commer was on a sound financial footing. Some smaller vehicles were introduced and soon a 10cwt van appeared based on the Hillman Minx car. The Rootes Group also acquired Karrier Motors in 1934, therefore in later years there was a certain amount of standardisation between the two makes. In 1935

Commer introduced its successful N range of normal and forward control for vans and lorries up to 5ton.

Just prior to the outbreak of World War 2 in 1939, the Superpoise (Q model) range was announced with five good-looking vehicles from 30cwt to 6tons with short bonnets. The engine protruded into the cab, but they proved popular with a wide variety of operators.

During World War 2, Commer produced over 20,000 vehicles for the fighting forces including Q4 (Superpoise) 4-5ton lorries (army rating 3ton), and tractive units for the 60ft long Queen Mary trailers used by the RAF for carrying aircraft fuselage.

Below:
A 1908 Commer loaded with apples in a Kentish orchard at the start of a journey to London.

Right:
A good load is being carried on this G2 model 2/2½ton lorry which is powered by a six-cylinder engine.

Below right:
A model G4 lorry built in 1931 for a 4ton payload, supplied to the Runcorn & Widnes Industrial Co-operative Society Ltd. A year later this model was redesignated GL4, being of lighter construction and available as normal or forward control versions.

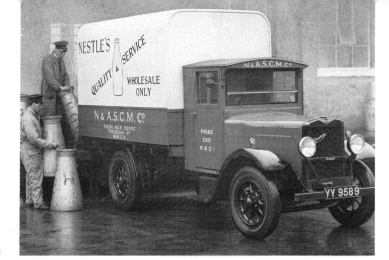

Top right:
The 1½ton Raider model was introduced in 1932 with a six-cylinder side valve engine of 22.6hp. The wheelbase was 10ft 6in. The model remained in production until 1935.

Centre right:
In the same year the Centaur model was announced for 2ton loads. The vehicle seen here is in Smithfield Market, Birmingham.

Below:
The 6/8cwt van of 1933 is based on the Hillman Minx car. The chassis cost £125, or the complete van £150.

Top left:
A forward control version of the Centaur 2tonner fitted with a loose tilt body and supplied new in 1934.

Centre left:
In 1935, Commer introduced the N series of vehicles ranging from 8cwt to 5ton. Here is a model N2 van with attractive signwriting.

Below:
The Commer Superpoise range succeeded the N series in 1939. The name Superpoise being inspired by the well balanced loading conditions of all the range, which were offered with petrol or diesel engines, forward or normal control, and with a wide variety of wheelbases. Shown here is 4/5ton lorry. The radiator, bonnet and cab was similar for most of the range.

Dennis

John Dennis started his business career building cycles in 1885, his younger brother, Raymond, soon joining the expanding concern. The next step was his Speed King motorcycles, and thus to motor cars. Dennis Brothers Ltd produced its first commercial vehicle in 1904 which was a 15cwt van with a four-cylinder 12hp engine. This vehicle probably had the patented Dennis worm gear rear axle, which, of course, dispensed with the chain drive used on practically all other vehicles. The first Dennis fire engine was built in 1908 for Bradford and Dennis have been famous for their various fire appliances ever since.

Dennis produced many different commercial vehicles using the White & Poppe four-cylinder T-head 40hp engine, and in 1913 produced its Model A subsidy 3½ton lorry (3ton army rating). Approximately 7,000 were produced.

In 1919 Dennis purchased White & Poppe Ltd which had supplied it and other manufacturers with engines. In the 1920s Dennis produced a large

number of lighter chassis of 30cwt, 2ton and 3ton capacity which were fitted with van and lorry bodies. Dennis also produced 6tonners, forward control models being introduced in 1927, and shortly afterwards the M type 12ton six-wheeler appeared, but this was not a success as only 36 had been sold by the time the model was taken out of their range in 1936. In 1934 the firm produced its own Dennis diesel engine.

One of the successes was the 40/45cwt chassis (called Ace for buses), which had the engine ahead of the front axle, giving a 'snout' effect and thus earning the nickname of 'Flying Pig'. A forward control version with the engine in the cab was also produced. In 1937 the Max 12ton six-wheel chassis was produced, also a 5ton four-wheeler, which after World War 2 was given the name Pax.

Dennis had many contracts with municipal authorities and the range of refuse collectors, gully emptiers, street washers, etc were very popular. Their fire appliances were in a class of their own, the only other rival of any size being Leyland.

During World War 2 Dennis produced vehicles for the government and essential civilian operators, as well as hundreds of trailer pumps for the fire services and undertook much subcontracted work including the assembly of Churchill tanks and the manufacture of gearboxes.

Below:
Introduced in 1926, the 4ton Dennis is a normal control (13ft 1½in or 14ft 1½in wheelbase) lorry powered by a Dennis four-cylinder petrol engine of 30hp. The vehicle shown here is a 1927 model beautifully preserved and often seen at rallies. *Stevens-Stratten Collection*

Above:
This 1931 3½ton Luton type pantechnicon has a body built by Clement, Butler & Cross.

Below:
A typical Dennis normal control 3tonner of the early 1930s. The body has a capacity of 1,000cu ft.

Top:
A 2ton van of 1931, which looked quite modern for the standards of its day. This particular vehicle was still in service at the end of World War 2, during which time it had been converted to gas power supplied from a bag mounted on the roof.

Above:
Dennis vehicles were always in favour with municipal authorities. This is one of two lorries supplied to the County Borough of East Ham to carry 3tons of household refuse.

Above:
This 7ton lorry was fitted with a Gardner six-cylinder diesel engine which due to its length necessitated a longer bonnet, giving a 'Bulldog' look to the vehicle. Note the single rear wheels on the third axle.

Below:
In 1935 the Dennis Ace was introduced to meet the competition from the mass production market in the 2/2½ton range. This is a 750gal multipurpose gully emptier, but this side view aptly describes the nickname given to the normal control Ace as the 'Flying Pig'!

Top right:
The forward control version of the Ace proved popular as it enabled the maximum space for a load within the minimum length of vehicle, also it was highly manoeuvrable. This was a 40/45cwt model used by a well-known parcels carrier.

Centre right:
At the end of 1935 a completely new Light Four 4tonner made an appearance using an elongated Ace radiator shell.

Below:
From its earliest days Dennis has always been one of the premier manufacturers of fire appliances. This is a Dennis Big Four featuring a six-cylinder petrol engine and a 800gal/min pump. It has transverse seating for the crew, which is safer than the Braidwood style where men sat facing outwards and could be flung off if the driver was over zealous in taking a corner! This is a 1935 machine with steel escape.

Dodge

The Dodge Brothers, John and Horace, produced the first motor car bearing their name in the USA in 1918, shortly afterwards producing some light commercial vehicles. These were imported into the UK, among the first being a 15cwt delivery van, which was popular with newspaper distributors and others as it was a fast vehicle.

The range was distributed by agents, but in 1923 Dodge Bros (GB) Ltd was formed and a small factory purchased in Stevenage Road, Fulham. Three years later this moved to larger premises near Park Royal, London NW10. The vehicles produced at this time consisted of a 15cwt van, a 1ton chassis, shortly joined by a 1½ton chassis, but all these were marketed with the Graham badge, one of the Dodge subsidiaries.

In 1928, the Dodge Bros concern was purchased by the Chrysler Corporation and the UK Dodge production moved to the Chrysler factory at Kew.

In 1933 the first British produced Dodge vehicles appeared, a 30cwt and 2ton and 4ton chassis, but still with the American built engine. From the mid-1930s the Dodge vehicles became a familiar sight on the British roads, particularly the 6ton tipper lorry, which was favoured by many contractors and sand and gravel merchants. The first truly all-British Dodge was produced in 1938 when it was fitted with a Perkins diesel engine. During the war the Kew factory was given over to the manufacture of components for aircraft production including the Halifax bombers.

Below:
A 30cwt chassis with van body by Wilsons (Kingston) Ltd with the whole of the side panelling in stainless steel.

Top right:
One of the early Graham Bros standard 15cwt delivery vans of 1928, fitted with a 24hp four-cylinder engine at a cost of £250 complete.

Centre right:
How appearances have changed in the space of 10 years! This is a 1937 Dodge 15cwt van used for public address work. It was used by a local rag and bone man to announce his presence.

Below:
A 1935 Dodge 3ton chassis with a three-compartment 1,500gal steel tank body.

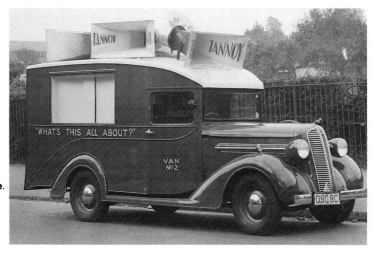

Above:
A 1939 Dodge 6ton chassis fitted with a tank body.

Left:
A 1938 Dodge 6ton truck carrying a car of the same make and year, seen outside the works at Kew.

ERF

This is a comparative newcomer to commercial vehicle production, although the initials ERF stand for Edwin Richard Foden, a member of the family who had been in the vehicle manufacturing business since 1888. A disagreement regarding the building of diesel engined lorries instead of the steam vehicles for which Foden was famous, resulted in Edwin starting his own company in 1933. In the first year 14 four-wheel, 6ton lorries with Gardner 4LW, 65bhp engines were produced. Various wheelbase options were offered, but all had four-speed crash gearboxes, a single-plate clutch and overhead worm rear axle. A year later a five-speed gearbox was optional.

A year after production commenced, the firm moved into the Sun Works at Sandbach (Cheshire), for the company soon found many customers as its products proved to be rugged and reliable. A 7ton version of the original model but fitted with a Gardner 5LW engine quickly appeared and in 1935 a 5ton four-wheeler, again with three different wheelbases (8ft 8in, 11ft 2in, or 12ft 8in) was available. All these models were of forward control layout and all were in production until the end of the war. A six-wheeler was offered in 1934 and the first of the ERF rigid eights appeared in 1936.

Left:
**Supplied to Forestry
Commission specifications
in 1941, these two artic
tractors with a wheelbase of
only 8ft 5in were fitted with
Gardner 5LW engines.**

Below left:
**This ERF four-wheel 6tonner
was supplied to Bulmers
Cider and is a good example
of the early models.**

Below:
**The standard ERF forward
control four-wheeled
6tonner.**

FWD

Four Wheel Drive of Milwaukee, USA, was formed in 1904, but was not known in this country until World War 1 when the US Army used FWD products in France. The vehicles were made with a track width of 4ft 8½in so they could quickly be used on a standard gauge railway line by merely changing the wheels.

After World War 1 many were offered by the government to the general public and were used by hauliers, forestry contractors and showmen who found the four-wheel drive extremely effective in obtaining traction on rough and muddy ground.

An English subsidiary was set up at Slough in 1921, first converting the original US Army models, and then producing lorries for general transport. In 1926, the British FWD, or Quad as it was sometimes known was produced with a larger 70bhp engine. Most of the models had a high cab sited over the engine.

A subsidiary company, Hardy Rail Motors, was formed for rail traction, but both companies found insufficient sales for such specialist vehicles and AEC took a controlling interest in the company in 1932. Some of the rail designs were incorporated in the AEC railcars which were produced shortly afterwards.

After the agreement with AEC, the FWD was redesigned to utilise more standard AEC components, and to avoid confusion with the American machines, the British vehicles were marketed under the name Hardy. Production seems to have ceased about 1936. FWDs were again imported into this country during World War 2, but were a vastly different looking vehicle.

Below:
A FWD chassis supplied to Norway and fitted with a Gorman centrifugal pump on the rear and searchlight mounted on a tank behind the driver's seat. This illustrates the height of the driving position.

Right:
A standard 4ton chassis fitted with a three-way hydraulic tipping body on pneumatic tyres.

A tipper with a later type of cab but on solid tyres.

Foden

Foden began making steam traction engines as far back as 1882, with regular production a couple of years later. The first Foden steam lorry was produced in 1900, and from that time the Foden name became synonymous with such vehicles, which continued to be manufactured until 1932.

In 1902 the steam lorry was a regular production at the Elworth Works, Sandbach, which was taken over from Plant & Hancock. The standard machines were overtype models, which had the cylinders and engine mounted on top of the boiler, with the flywheels just below the steering handle; the steersman half standing in a fairing (or 'scuttle') on the near-side. These wagons had a load capacity of 5ton and a wheelbase of 14ft 10in. They remained in production until 1923.

In 1920 an improved overtype made its appearance, again for a 6ton payload, but with many improvements — both crew members now being accommodated in the open type cab. Boiler pressure was 200lb/sq in for the compound engine with steam jacketed cylinders of 4¼in (high pressure) and 7in (low pressure), both having a 7in stroke. Three wheelbases were available — 10ft 6in for tractors; 13ft 10in for a tipper; and 14ft 9in for the standard chassis.

The crippling taxation and other restrictions imposed on steam driven vehicles, plus the increasing efficiency of the petrol and diesel engines, caused the death of the steam lorry, so, reluctantly, Foden turned its attention to diesel lorries. The first of the new production — a 6ton lorry — was supplied in July 1931, and the last steam vehicle was produced in 1933.

The first diesel vehicle had a Gardner engine fitted and thus started a long association between the two companies. All Foden models were of the forward control layout and the range prior to World War 2 was from 6ton rigid four-wheelers to 15ton eight-wheelers, many of the models having the distinctive curved-fronted cab. The coding for the vehicles denoted engine type and payload — DG5/15 would be a DG model fitted with a Gardner 5LW engine to carry a 15ton load. Foden also made a number of diesel powered timber tractors.

During the war Foden produced 1,750 vehicles for the War Department, 770 Crusader and Centaur tanks and over 7½ million 20mm shells.

Below:
An early Foden steam wagon of 1910 with steel wheels, tyres and brake blocks. Note the maximum speed on the chassis frame!

Above right:
The 5ton Foden steamer was introduced in 1902 and continued in production until 1923. This beautifully-restored example dates from 1916. *Stevens-Stratten Collection*

Below right:
This C type was built in 1922 and has attended many rallies since it was preserved. Note the front axle suspension.
Stevens-Stratten Collection

Top:
**One of the last Foden steam lorries was this
1931 Speed-12 undertype 10/12ton tipper built
to carry farm manure and chemicals. The water
supply is in the tank behind the cab.**

Above:
**The first diesel lorry produced by Fodens — the
R type — in 1931. Fitted with a Gardner 5L2 oil
engine, it carried a 6ton load.**
Stevens-Stratten Collection

54

By 1933 Fodens had a production line for the 4/6ton lorry shown here.

Below:
A type DG5/7½ lorry with a body length of 16ft. The first figure of the model type was the number of cylinders (ie 5LW), the second figure was the payload in tons.

Top:
A 10ton six-wheeler for 12ton loads.

Above:
This 1937 example represents the ultimate in design for a 15ton eight-wheeler.

Ford

Henry Ford is reputed to have said that his customers could have any colour for their vehicle, as long as it was black! The American-built vehicles were imported from 1904, and reached such numbers that an assembly plant was set up at Trafford Park, Manchester in 1911. In 1911 the famous Model T with a load capacity of 7cwt was available, and shortly afterwards the updated and 'stretched' Model TT for 1ton loads was made. The Model T continued in production until 1927 — a period of 16 years.

The Model A for 15cwt loads and the AA and AAF for 20-30cwt were in production from 1928-1933, both models using the four-cylinder, 40bhp engine and four-speed gearbox. Wire wheels were later replaced by a disc type.

The works at Dagenham commenced production in 1931 when the B (15-25cwt) and the BB and BBF (2ton) were made at first using the same engine, although shortly afterwards a 65bhp V8 engine was introduced, but this had a problem with high oil consumption.

From 1935 models were called 'Fordson' and semi-forward control was available on certain models, the range being from 2ton to 5ton, fitted with a four-cylinder 24hp engine or the 30hp V8 engine. The 5cwt van was based on the 8hp car, using some of the same body components. Two interesting models were the Surrey and Sussex six-wheelers, the latter having a double drive rear axle.

The 7V series were introduced from 1937 for payloads of 2ton to 5ton with a choice of different wheelbases. Perkins diesel engines could also be fitted as an optional extra. Hydraulic brakes became standard on all models from 1939 and from March of that year all the Dagenham-built vehicles were named Thames.

During World War 2, Ford produced a large number of the 7V series for the government, some being used as the basis for a Home Office fire appliance. Army vehicles included the type WOT 15cwt truck, and the 3ton 4×4 general service lorry.

A 1923 model T Ford flat truck, now preserved and seen at a rally.
Stevens-Stratten Collection

Above:
In 1932 the Woolwich dealers for Ford, Herwin Canny & Co, supplied 10 Ford AAF models to a firm of road haulage contractors.

Below:
Another Ford model A with bodywork for carrying livestock or market garden produce.

Top:
This stylish van is a Fordson 15cwt of 1936.

Above:
This prewar 3ton market gardener's truck sold for £335.

Left:

During World War 2 many thousands of these Ford 10cwt vans were in use as mobile canteens serving the armed forces and civilians. A great number were donated and run by voluntary services.

Below left:

A mobile kitchen on a 2ton chassis in 1942.

Below:

A wartime Ford chassis with horsebox body.

Bottom:

Towards the end of World War 2 some 2ton chassis were available, identified by the wire mesh radiator grille.

Fowler

John Fowler & Company (Leeds) Ltd was registered in 1886 and manufactured steam traction engines. Fowler built steam-powered lorries from 1924 until 1935 and during this time a total of 117 were constructed, but they were not entirely successful due to steaming problems. The exception was the Fowler gulley emptiers, which latterly formed a large part of Fowler's production, so it would seem that providing frequent stops were made, steam pressure could be maintained.

In 1931 Fowler introduced its first diesel-engined lorry, which was a semi-forward control model for 6/7ton payloads. This, and the following six-wheeled 10-12ton vehicle, had a massive frontal appearance, but they do not appear to have proved popular with the road haulage industry. The company fitted both models with its own oil engine of six-cylinders, of 4⅜in diameter by 7in stroke, with the pistons having a patented cavity.

Fowler ceased production of goods vehicles in 1935, concentrating on a range of agricultural tractors and machinery which had been manufactured since approximately 1910.

Above:
A 1931 Fowler 6/7ton heavy-oil engined lorry and trailer.

Right:
A typical Fowler with a heavy load. Does it look like an over-fat Boxer dog?

Garner

Henry Garner Ltd started in 1909, when the name was changed from Moseley Motor Works, which had commenced two years earlier. Production was spasmodic to say the least, but fortunes changed in 1927 when the name was changed to Garner Motors Ltd.

A large range was produced, although the sales figures may not have been very high. The most popular vehicle appears to have been the model 4JO, introduced in 1931, for a 4ton payload. This was powered by a 22.4hp four-cylinder petrol engine, with a choice of four wheelbases.

In 1933 Garner was merged with Sentinel and the 4JO model was produced at the Shrewsbury works until 1936. A very modern-looking vehicle was produced with a radiator grille which was similar to that used by Sentinel itself when it commenced production of its own diesel lorries in 1946. Just prior to World War 2 in 1939, the firm made some Garner-Straussler specialist military vehicles which were fitted with twin Ford V8 engines.

Left:
A 2½ton chassis with a 13ft 8in wheelbase with a van body of 1,030cu ft capacity and an interior length of 17ft by 8ft height.

Below:
A 1932 2ton Garner model AB dropside lorry. The wheelbase is 11ft long and the body length is 10ft 4in by 6ft 6in wide with 16in sides.

Above:
The model JO6 was a 4ton chassis with a 12ft 5in wheelbase. The body could carry a mixed load of 10, 12 or 17gal milk churns — hence the upper deck on the front part for carrying the 10gal churns. A six-cylinder 36hp engine was fitted.

Below:
A six-wheeled model TW60s mobile public address van which had a six-cylinder 56.6hp engine and a 4ton load capacity.

Garrett

Richard Garrett & Co Ltd had its headquarters at Leiston in the heart of the Suffolk farmland, and therefore it is not surprising that production centred on agricultural machinery and traction engines, for which the firm was well known and respected. Among its successes in this field must be mentioned the Suffolk Punch tractor.

The first Garrett steam lorry was produced in 1904 and the company entered the field of battery-electric vehicles in 1921, also making some trolleybuses in 1928. The first Garrett diesel engined lorry appeared in 1930, fitted with a Blackstone six-cylinder engine.

During the 1930s the company became part of the Beyer Peacock Group and the production of road vehicles was slowly phased out so that by 1939 the works were making other engineering products.

Below:
A beautifully restored Garrett six-wheeled steam wagon, few examples of which now exist. *R. G. Pratt*

Bottom:
The first diesel lorry built by Garrett was in fact a steam wagon with a diesel engine and radiator placed in the front of the chassis.

Gilford

The Gilford Motor Co Ltd of High Wycombe started off as E. B. Horne & Company of Holloway Road, London N7 in 1926 when it was converting war surplus vehicles. Just over a year later the company moved to larger premises at Bellfields, High Wycombe, where it began to produce a range of buses and coaches, which were popular with their operators, and many saw a long life. The petrol engines were originally of USA design and incorporated many components imported from that country; in fact the Gilford used many components from other manufacturers. The chassis was noted for the fitting of Gruss auxiliary air springs to the front suspension which assisted comfortable riding qualities.

The range of Gilford goods vehicles was not so large, nor so popular, as the buses and coaches, and experiments with the four-wheel drive system with the introduction of the Tangye oil engine were almost a disaster, certainly in the early stages.

The AS6 model, for small passenger vehicles, was used for goods vehicles from 1930-1936, also the DF6 model. It had a six-cylinder petrol engine of 31.5hp and a low underslung rear axle. Vacuum servo assisted rear wheel brakes were fitted. One of this type has been preserved, in fact it is the only known Gilford goods vehicle now in existence. The company went out of business in 1937.

Below:
A 1930 Gilford SF6 model 2½/3ton lorry powered by a six-cylinder 85hp engine.

Above:
Again normally used as a coach chassis this 168SD is carrying a 1,000gal Thompson Bros (Bilston) Ltd tank body.

Below:
A 1931 model AS6 van originally owned by the Danish Bacon Co and now preserved. The chassis was normally used for 20-seat coaches, but in this case it carried a 50cwt payload.

Guy

Guy Motors Ltd was formed in 1914 at Fallings Park, Wolverhampton by Sydney S. Guy, following his resignation as Works Manager for Sunbeam Motor Car Co Ltd. The first vehicle to be produced was a 30cwt lorry, with a then revolutionary device — now called an overdrive! World War 1 intervened with the production of other vehicles until 1920, when a farmer's lorry was produced fitted with 'spud' wheels for traversing muddy ground. An articulated lorry followed in 1922, a battery-electric refuse collector a year later, and then followed a variety of vehicles, all of normal control.

The turning point for Guy commercial vehicles came with the introduction in 1933 of the Wolf, normal control 2ton model. The Vixen 3/4ton followed and a year later Guy had another triumph with the Otter 6ton chassis, which weighed under 2½ton fully equipped.

It was in 1934 that the famous radiator cap with the Red Indian head and the slogan 'Feathers in our Cap' first appeared, which was to be the company's symbol until its demise.

Civilian vehicle production ceased in 1938 as

Guy took up urgent government contracts for military vehicles, which continued throughout the war. A variety of military material was manufactured, including on the vehicle side the six-wheeled lorries, the well-known Quad-Ant gun tractors, and even a light tank. However, in 1941 the company were allowed to produce some vehicles for hauliers with special MoWT licences. These were the Vix-ant, a basic Vixen with many Guy Ant (a military 15cwt) parts, including the bonnet and radiator, which were of distinctive, and certainly 'utility' appearance.

Below:
A 1922 Guy model J 25cwt truck powered by a 17hp engine and now preserved, having delivered coal for 29 years.

Right:
Two 1932 Guy 30/40cwt model UW vans. Incidentally this operator had a fleet of 23 Guy vehicles — so they kept them running!

Below right:
A 1936 J type lorry.

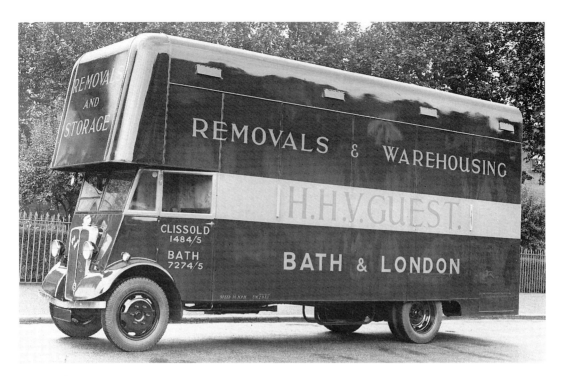

Above left:
A 1935 Guy Wolf 2ton van with four-cylinder (90mm by 130mm) 50hp engine. The wheelbase is 10ft 6in and the overall length is 16ft 1½in, the body length being 9ft 6in.

Left:
This Otter 6½ton lorry was supplied in 1939.

Above:
The Vixen 3/4ton chassis with pantechnicon body of maximum size was an ideal vehicle for removal and storage work.

Below:
The 1940-dated Wolf normal and forward control Vixen side by side.

Halley

Halley Industrial Motors, which started as the Glasgow Motor Lorry Co, was first registered in 1906, producing both steam and petrol driven vehicles. The company won both gold and silver awards with their two-cylinder, 30cwt and 2ton models in the 1907 trials which lasted for 17 days. The early engines were made by Tylor, but from 1910 Halley began making its own 25hp and 35hp four-cylinder engines, plus a large six-cylinder unit which developed 50bhp.

The pre-1914 output was considerable and Halley was considered to be among the big 10 motor vehicle manufacturers. The firm were particularly successful with the manufacture of fire appliances, which were in use by many Scottish brigades.

From 1914-18, Halley made shells and only a few vehicles were produced. When peace returned the company produced its new P series 3½ton (or 29/35seat) chassis with a six-cylinder engine. At first this proved to be a good seller, but the depression of the period had its effect and sales began to slump. A 2ton S model was also produced, but this never sold in great numbers.

The early vehicles had a radiator with a shape similar to those on the Associated Daimler vehicles of c1926, but with the name Halley cast in the header tank. Later models had a pointed radiator.

In 1927 the company went into liquidation and re-emerged with the name changed to Halley Motors Ltd. Unfortunately, sales slowly declined yet again, and production ceased in 1935, when the firm finally closed and the works at Yoker were acquired by Albion, who used the premises as a packing plant for CKD export models, and also as a servicing plant.

Right:
A 2½ton Halley van of 1929 which is now preserved and seen here on the HCVS London-Brighton run in 1969. *S. W. Stevens-Stratten*

Below:
A 2ton tipping lorry of 1930.

Hallford

Hallford vehicles were produced from 1906 by the well known and long established firm of J. & E. Hall, of Dartford, Kent, the name being a corruption of Hall and Dartford. The firm produced a 25hp four-cylinder engine using Saurer patents, and early success came in 1907 in the RAC Commercial Motor Trials when a 3ton lorry was awarded a gold medal plus a special diploma. Hallford then used its own design of engine in a range of vehicles from 35cwt to 5ton.

In its early days, the company undertook many experiments with petrol-electric traction for Thomas Tilling, which were later incorporated into the Tilling Stevens vehicles built at Maidstone. A large number of these were buses, but a few commercials were produced under the Hallford banner. Hallford continued some vehicle production under its own name, and during World War 1 was responsible for the manufacture of a large number of chassis for army lorries, of conventional design for the period.

After the war, the firm closed its motor manufacturing activities in 1923, rather than use capital for costly new designs and development in a competitive market, where its present models were outdated. Hallford products were distinguished by a bonnet top which sloped down to a pointed radiator top.

Below:
The Hallford 1914 WD type 3tonner, now restored and seen at the first HCVC rally in 1958 at the Spurrier works, Leyland.

Karrier

Clayton & Company of Huddersfield started Karrier Motors Ltd in 1904, although the name was not used until 1920. The first range of vehicles was designated, sensibly, the A-type, which had the driver sitting in a high position above the engine. Payloads from 2ton to 5½ton could be supplied, all with Tylor engines of various sizes. Chain drive was standard, as were cone clutches.

One of the first vehicles of the newly-named company was the K-type; this was a normal control vehicle of which there were five models in the range, which was produced until 1931. The H-type was a four-wheeler for 2ton payloads with either normal or forward control configuration, which was introduced in 1923 and remained in production until the early 1930s; the GH4 being a variation for 4ton payloads. In 1929 the ZA model proved popular as it was a small normal control chassis for a 25cwt load.

One of Karrier's many contributions to the industry was the development work it undertook in conjunction with the London Midland & Scottish Railway for a replacement of the horse and the Karrier Cob three-wheeled tractor was the result. This was introduced in 1931 and continued in production until 1938, being powered by a Jowett 7hp engine.

The Karrier Motor Company was taken over by the Rootes Group in 1934 when production was moved from Huddersfield to Luton being allied to the Commer concern, which by then was also under Rootes control.

The CK range, introduced in 1935, proved very successful and some models continued in production until 1952. Another prewar success was the Bantam, a forward control, small wheeled, vehicle for 2/3ton loads, often being used as the chassis for refuse collectors and other municipal vehicles, as well as a short-wheelbase version being extensively used as the motive power for semi-trailers. This again continued in production after the war, albeit with a modernised frontal appearance. During World War 2 Karrier produced army lorries, and other munitions work.

Below:
Two Karrier 3½ton Victor models of 1932 fitted with lightweight bodies and powered by a four-cylinder (95mm by 140mm) 47hp engine.

Right:
In 1933 this 50cwt lorry with a Dorman-Ricardo heavy oil engine is undergoing a test run near Calver.

Below right:
One of the early Bantam 2tonners of 1934. This tipping lorry had a four-cylinder (69mm by 90mm) 11.8hp engine.

Below:
**One of the successful CK3 models. This
15cu yd van was fitted with a moving floor.**

Bottom:
**Another CK3, on motorised refuse collection in
1936.**

Above:
The Bantam 2tonner was popular with many operators and used to carry a variety of loads. Here is part of a fleet of a well known goods and parcels carrier.

Below:
One of the very early Karrier Cob mechanical horses in 1931.

Right and below:
One of the original and primary ideas for the introduction of the mechanical horse — complete compatibility for trailer haulage by horse or mechanical transport.

Bottom:
A Karrier Colt three-wheeler for light loads. Manoeuvring in congested areas was easy. This photograph was taken in 1933.

Lacre

When the company was founded in 1902 in Long Acre, in the Covent Garden area of London, the thoroughfare was known as the street of car dealers. Lacre was a contraction of Long Acre.

The firm produced cars and its 25cwt, 16hp van appeared in 1904 after which Lacre continued with the production of small vans, achieving considerable success with sales to London retail stores.

In 1910 the company commenced production of commercial vehicles at a new factory in Letchworth, Hertfordshire, where a range extending from 10cwt to 10ton payload was made. Some of the larger vehicles saw service in France during World War 1.

The model 'O' was introduced in 1909 which was a highly successful normal control 2/2½ton payload chassis with a wheelbase of 12ft fitted with a four-cylinder engine developing 30hp. A three-speed gearbox coupled to a cone clutch and a double chain-driven rear axle was also standard. By being updated, the basic 'O' model continued in production until 1935.

A 30/35cwt model appeared in 1921 with a

wheelbase of 10ft 6in and in the same year the larger model was given the option of a 38hp engine. In 1922 a 4tonner was produced known as the Colonial type or 'N' model.

The firm also made its name with the design and production of three-wheel roadsweepers, the single wheel at the rear being chain-driven from a Dorman petrol engine of 11.8hp. Production of these strange looking machines started in 1919 and finished in 1936.

Due to financial difficulties the original company was wound up in 1928, but was reconstituted immediately with the title changed to Lacre Lorries Ltd, establishing new works at Welwyn Garden City. It is worth recalling that the designer for Lacre Lorries was J. S. Drewry — see under Shelvoke & Drewry.

Below:
A 1913 Lacre model O 2ton van, which saw service in World War 1 has been faithfully restored and preserved. Seen here on the 1972 HCVS Brighton Run. *S. W. Stevens-Stratten*

Latil

Latil was a French vehicle manufacturer established since 1904, whose products were originally marketed under the name Blum-Latil. Latil Industrial Vehicles Ltd was formed in the UK in 1924, but from 1932 vehicles were produced under licence by Shelvoke & Drewry. Latil products were then given the subsidiary name of Traulier. Most of the production consisted of four-wheel drive tractors, with an auxiliary gearbox. Latil's own petrol engine was originally fitted, but in later years alternative power units were available, usually a Meadows diesel. It would appear that one of the drawbacks of the Latil was the large turning circle required to undertake a 360° turn.

Latil made several tractors for railway shunting, utilising four small flanged steel wheels which acted as guides on the railway track, the power coming from the normal road wheels which rested on the rail surface, for the front and rear track of Latil tractors was the same as the standard railway gauge.

Right:
A forestry tractor supplied in 1935 and exhibited at the Royal Agricultural Show in Bristol the following year. Fitted with a winch, the stakes on the wheels could be folded down for extra grip on muddy ground. It had a four-cylinder petrol engine of 20.1hp (RAC rating).

One of the experiments of the Shelvoke & Drewry regime was the adaptation of this Traulier tractor for road/rail use in 1936. As the track of the vehicle was the same as the railway gauge (4ft 8½in) the small steel wheels could be lowered to act as guides.

Leyland

Leyland Motors Ltd, which for the period covered by this book was one of the largest commercial vehicle manufacturers, began its existence as the Lancashire Steam Motor Company in 1896, building steam wagons, its first being a 30cwt, fitted with a 10-14hp two-cylinder compound engine, fed from an oil-fired boiler. This was followed by a more conventional 3tonner and thus they progressed, so that by 1904 the company had produced 72 steam lorries or buses. Steam-powered vehicles were taken out of the Leyland sales literature in 1926. The first experimental petrol engined lorry was made in 1904, but it was not a success; however a year later the company was producing petrol buses for London as well as some lorries.

In 1907 the name was changed to Leyland Motors Limited and a range of heavy vehicles (nothing under 3½ton) was now offered with either steam or petrol propulsion. Success came with the introduction of the 3ton lorry which became known as the RAF type, as during World War 1 nearly 6,000 were produced, the model being continued until 1926. Many different models were produced during the 1920s.

The year 1929 saw Leyland with a completely new range, all given names of animals — Badger, Buffalo, Bison, Bull, etc, which became almost household words in the commercial transport field.

In 1931 the Cub made its appearance, a highly successful 2tonner built at the works at Kingston-upon-Thames. This lightweight was fitted with a six-cylinder engine and had hydraulic brakes acting on all four wheels.

In 1933 Leyland was able to offer an oil engine as an alternative to the petrol engine for its range and the former soon became popular as a more economic unit.

Leyland also offered several fire appliances, having an agreement with Metz the German turntable ladder manufacturers, and with Dennis were the major builders of fire appliances prior to World War 2.

During the hostilities, Leyland was fully occupied, manufacturing the Convanter tank, engines for the Matilda tank, assembling Churchill tanks and also producing high explosive and incendiary bombs (over 11 million of these) and 20mm shells. Some utility bus chassis and a few 10ton Hippo lorries were also produced.

Below:
A Leyland steamer of c1905 alongside a model X of 1908. Both vehicles are now preserved.

Above:
**A close-up view of the steam lorry shown on
the previous page.** *Stevens-Stratten Collection*

Below:
**A Leyland of c1921 which was still in service
27 years later.**

Above right:
**The P type 6tonner of 1920s was an early form
of forward control with the driver perched high
above the engine.**

Below right:
One of the early Cub models of 1931.

Above left:
A Terrier six-wheeler of 1933 used on trunk work. This was also the name given to an Army type six-wheeler during the war.

Left:
A Leyland Badger TA4 of 1932, for a 4ton payload.

Above:
A forward control Badger 5tonner of 1934.

Below:
This 1935 Beaver TC10 6ton chassis has an ebonite lined tank body for the carrying of hydrochloric acid. A 32.4hp diesel engine is fitted.

Above:
A Hippo six-wheeler of 1936.

Below:
The Lynx 5/6ton four-wheeler was introduced in 1937. A six-cylinder petrol or oil engine could be fitted.

McCurd

W. A. McCurd was an automobile engineer, who is believed to have been a 'one-man business' until 1913, when a limited company was formed and commercial vehicles were produced in premises at Slough, Bucks until 1927.

In 1912 a large 5ton chassis was produced and was made until 1914, with a four-cylinder engine of 32.4hp, the normal four-speed crash gearbox and cone clutch. Unusually at this time, a choice of worm or bevel drive was available for the rear axle.

One example is preserved.

Below:
Believed to be the only survivor, this 1913 McCurd van is being prepared for the start of an HCVS event. *Stevens-Stratten Collection*

Maudslay

The origins of the Maudslay concern go back to 1833 when Maudslay & Field became an engineering partnership and achieved some fame by improving a Gurney steam vehicle. The Maudslay family name became well known in many fields of engineering and the Maudslay Motor Company was formed in 1903 to manufacture cars and light vans. In 1907 a 3ton lorry was produced, with a 30/40hp four-cylinder engine, which won a gold medal in a RAC Industrial Motor Trial. In 1912 a range of 30cwt, 3ton and 5ton chassis were produced. From 1914-18 some vehicles were made, but Maudslay concentrated mainly on parts for aero engines.

At the 1921 Motor Show a 3/4ton, 4/5ton, 5/6ton and 6/7ton with a 50hp engine were on display. However, the manufacture of buses and coaches became a primary function in the 1920s and 1930s, but in 1929 a 10ton six-wheeled commercial vehicle chassis with a four-cylinder engine, rated at 75hp, was produced. This appears to have saved a somewhat ailing company, and in 1933 the Mogul (Mk 1) four-wheeled, 6ton lorry, but rated in the 4ton taxation class, was built. This was fitted with a Gardner engine.

The financial slump finally hit Maudslay, but in 1939 a completely new range of vehicles, designed by Siegfried Sperling (an Austrian who had recently left his home country) and fitted with Gardner engines, had been produced for the Commercial Motor Show of that year, which unfortunately had to be cancelled due to World War 2. This new range appeared after the war and was successful.

During the war, Maudslay produced the Mogul and Militant two-axle vehicles plus much military equipment, opening a 'shadow' factory at Alcester, and undertaking much subcontracted work.

Above right:
A long wheelbase four-wheeled Maudslay.

Far right:
A Maudslay with trailing third axle about to negotiate a ford on a road test in 1930.

Right:
A 10tonner of 1931, again with a trailing rear axle.

Above:
A similar vehicle to that on the previous page, with a van body which gives some idea of the amount of goods which could be carried.

Below:
The new Mogul introduced in 1938 for 7½ton payloads had the option of a four-cylinder petrol or diesel engine.

Above:
Two earlier Mogul models of 1939. One wonders how Hurst & Payne allocated their fleet numbers!

Below:
The Merlin II was a 6ton vehicle introduced in 1940 with a wheelbase of 11ft 6in and supplied with a four-cylinder petrol engine.

Below:
Another Merlin with platform body of 15ft length supplied in 1939.

Bottom:
This Mogul 7tonner was delivered in 1940 for essential civilian use.

Morris Commercial

William Morris, later Lord Nuffield, had been producing cars for many years and some light vans had been built on car chassis from 1913, but it was not until 1924 that his company entered into the commercial vehicle market.

The first vehicle to have the Morris Commercial badge was a 1ton lorry which with small updates, lasted in production until 1939. It was designated the 'T' model, with a wheelbase of 10ft 2in powered by a 13.9hp side-valve engine as used in one of the car range. Then followed the 'L' type for 8cwt payloads, but this was soon increased to 10cwt, then 12cwt and finally 15cwt as the L2 model in 1930. An 11.9hp engine was first used, but this was succeeded by the trusted 13.9hp engine in the L2 model.

The 'D' type of 1927 heralded the entry of Morris into the six-wheeled field for 30cwt and 2ton loads. At one time Morris could claim to be the largest producer of six-wheeled chassis, and their use by the army was soon firmly established.

Taking over the old Wolseley Works at Adderley Park, Birmingham in 1933, Morris introduced a range of heavier vehicles, starting with the 'P' type or Leader 2½tonner (soon uprated to 3ton) with a 22.4hp petrol engine.

The 'C' type was a new design for 1934 with semi-forward or normal control, while the Leader had the new design of cab and was again re-rated for 3/4ton. The 'C' range was very popular and sold well in all its variants. This applied also the the 'CV' range introduced from 1937, which was also known as Equiload, distinguished by its vee-shaped radiator front.

Morris also produced bus chassis and provided some fire appliances. The company's sales to the Post Office and large companies made most commercial vehicle manufacturers envious, and, perhaps, justified their slogan 'British to the Backbone'. During World War 2 Morris produced large numbers of vehicles for the Armed Forces.

Below:
A 1927 van with electric lights and opening windscreen.

Above:
A demonstration 7cu yd refuse collection vehicle.

Below:
With a specially treated body and chassis to resist the corrosive effects of salt, this six-wheeler with fully articulated rear axles was supplied to ICI in 1938.

The pleasing looks of the 1938 Equiload is well shown in this photograph of a 5ton chassis with 1,500gal petrol tank body by the Aluminium Plant & Vessel Co.

In 1938 the semi-forward control Equiload model was announced. This is the long wheelbase version.

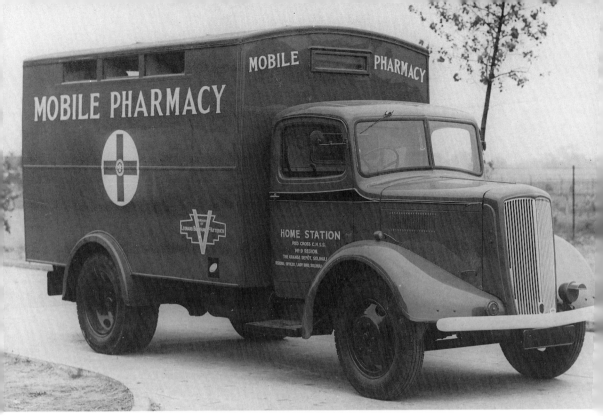

Top:
A wartime 3ton van. Would you like to drive this in the blackout with these lights?

Above:
A Morris Equiload 25cwt van of 1938 which again shows the clean lines and balanced look of the vehicle.

Pagefield

Pagefield was the name given to commercial road vehicles manufactured by Walker Brothers of Pagefield Iron Works, Wigan, Lancs, a firm which was formed in 1904, for general engineering, but produced a 2ton lorry in 1907. By 1913 Walker Brothers was producing a subsidy 4ton lorry using a 42hp Dorman engine, and 519 were built for the services. Known as the N model it was produced, with some updates, until 1931. A 5ton model, basically similar, was made in 1922.

In the mid-1920s and 1930s Pagefield became renowned for a unique refuse collecting scheme, whereby horse drawn trucks, with small diameter wheels, made the house-to-house collections, and when the trucks were full, they were winched up ramps on the back of a special Pagefield lorry and driven to the refuse tip. The lorry deposited an empty truck for the horse to continue the collection. Thus large towns needed only a few licensed lorries for this service.

In 1930 Pagefield produced some mobile cranes for the London Midland & Scottish and the London & North Eastern Railway companies, using Dorman engines. Later, Tilling Stevens petrol electric units supplied the power for transmission and lifting etc.

One of the company's popular models was the six-wheel, 12ton Plantagenet chassis which was introduced in 1931 and powered by a Gardner 6LW diesel engine.

A similar 4ton design on a four-wheel chassis was named the Pompian; there was also a 6ton Pathfinder and Pegasix was the name given to a trailing axle six-wheeler. A 6/7ton Paladin model followed and this range continued on a limited basis until World War 2. During the war years, Pagefield made shells and sections for the Mulberry Harbour project, plus a number of special cranes.

Below:
A Pagefield Plantagenet six-wheel 12ton lorry of 1932. A five-cylinder oil engine was fitted.

Above:
The Prodigy was introduced in 1932 for 3/3½ton loads and from 1936 was available with a choice of petrol or diesel engine.

Centre right:
An example of the Pagefield refuse collection system. The trailer has been winched on to the lorry for the journey to the tip, but is drawn by a horse when making house-to-house collections.

Bottom right:
A Pegasix supplied to J. Lyons in 1934 and powered by a Gardner 5LW diesel engine. The 6ton payload could be increased by 4ton if a trailer was hauled.

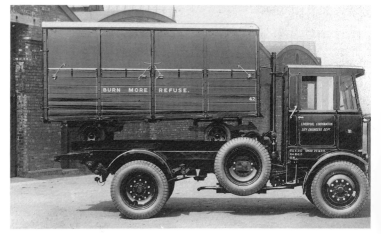

Peerless

This is not really a British company in the true sense of the word, for the vehicles in the UK were wartime imports from America and many thousands were used in France. After World War 1 they were reconditioned by Slough Lorries & Components Ltd from whom, in 1920, a 5ton lorry could be purchased for as little as £255. The company then became Peerless Trading Company and finally Peerless Lorries Ltd.

The Trader was a normal control lorry, built from available parts, but from 1925 was purpose built. All the parts were imported from the Peerless Motor Company of Cleveland, Ohio. Many of the vehicles had pneumatic tyres at the front, but solids on the rear; chain drive being used for the transmission.

Above:
The Peerless Tradersix 90 with pneumatic tyres on the front and solids on the rear, allegedly giving better adhesion. Note the short drive chain to the rear axle.

Below:
Another Tradersix. Note hydraulic tipping arrangement.

Raleigh and Reliant

The Raleigh Cycle Company of Nottingham produced a three-wheeled light delivery van in 1930, which was designed by T. L. Williams and derived from the James Karryall. The first model, the LDV (Light Delivery Van) used a 598cc single-cylinder, side valve, air-cooled engine, and had a payload capacity of 5cwt. The model was

Below:
A 1934 Raleigh three-wheeled 8cwt van which is now preserved and seen on the HCVS London-Brighton Run in 1986.
S. W. Stevens-Stratten

produced for three years when it was superseded by the Safety Seven for 8cwt loads, fitted with a two-cylinder 742cc air-cooled engine, and the wheelbase was increased from 5ft 6in to 6ft 8in. Production ceased in 1935.

The Reliant Engineering Company of Tamworth produced the three-wheeled van, also designed by T. L. Williams, in 1936. This was a 7cwt model with single-cylinder engine, but was soon followed by a two-cylinder, 10cwt version. In 1939 a four-cylinder engine of 749cc was fitted to both 8cwt and 10cwt models which remained standard for many years.

Scammell

The birth of Scammell vehicles goes back to a pioneering and experimental articulated lorry made in 1921 in Spitalfields, London, when the idea of using a four-wheel tractor coupled to a two-wheeled semi-trailer became a reality. The advantage was a longer load space, plus greater payload capacity, which could be achieved without exceeding the legal axle weights.

The manufacturer of this innovation was G. Scammell & Nephewe Ltd., an old established firm of wheelwrights and coachbuilders. The experiment was successful so Scammell Lorries Ltd was formed a year later and moved to a factory at Tolpits Lane, Watford, where production began in earnest.

The original tractor units were chain-driven and many semi-trailer tankers were produced for carrying bulk liquids such as petrol and oil. The early tractive units were powered by 63bhp four-cylinder side valve engines. In 1927 Scammell introduced the Pioneer six-wheeled tractor unit with a highly flexible suspension whereby there could be a 2ft vertical movement of each wheel and the chassis remained level.

In 1929 a four-wheel rigid vehicle was introduced for 6ton payloads, and two years later a rigid-six which proved popular for 10ton loads. Chain drive continued on the tractive units for some years to come.

Scammell was also famous for its three-wheeled tractive units — the mechanical horse — which was introduced in 1932. This vehicle was to revolutionise short haul collection and delivery services for the railway companies and for many municipal authorities for refuse collection. During World War 2 Scammell made many Pioneer tractors for tank recovery work, plus trailer pumps for the fire service.

Below:
Scammells have been used for articulated petrol tankers since the early days of the company. Here is a 1930 model.

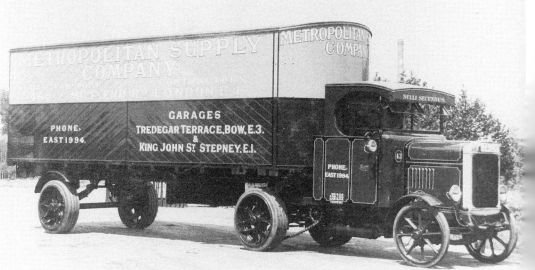

Top:
The Rigid-Six of 1932 6×2, (meaning that only the first of the two rear axles is driven). From 1933 this could be offered with an oil engine as an alternative.

Above:
A c1921 chain-driven tractor and semi-trailer for the carriage of meat.
Courtesy Andrew Meadows

Above right:
A 1933 Scammell tanker.

Right:
One of the early Scammell Pioneers undergoing tests in 1932. This shows a good example of axle articulation at front and rear.

Left:
A Rigid-Four, introduced in 1929 for 6ton payloads. This was one of the first Scammell vehicles to dispense with chain drive. It was powered by the usual 80bhp engine and this is a 1931 model with a special concrete mixer body.

Bottom left:
The rigid eight-wheeled 15/16ton chassis was introduced in 1937 and remained available, virtually unchanged, until the arrival of the Routeman in 1960. The standard power unit was the Gardner 6LW diesel engine.

Below:
One of the two 100tonners built in 1929 and 1931. Originally powered by the 80bhp engine, they were subsequently converted to a Gardner 6LW. It is seen here traversing the level crossing at Warmley with a stator of Metropolitan-Vickers manufacture.

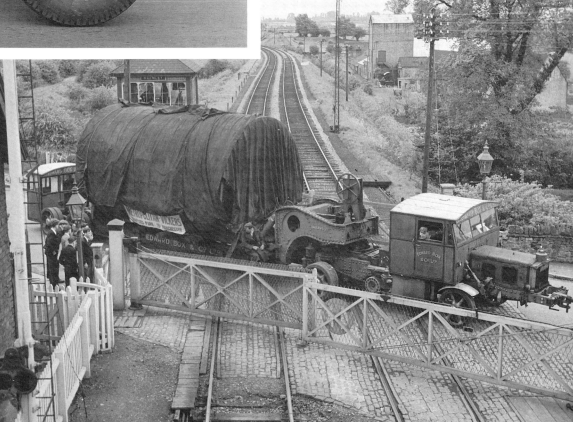

Top:
An early example of the Scammell mechanical horse.

Above:
A 6ton mechanical horse in 1941.

Seddon

A relative newcomer to the commercial vehicle manufacturers, Foster & Seddon Ltd, of Salford, Lancashire, commenced production in 1937 with a 6ton payload vehicle which weighed under 50cwt unladen. For the previous 18 years the firm had been engaged in the repair and maintenance side of the business.

This first production vehicle was a forward control, four wheeled, 6tonner with a platform body and fitted with the standard Perkins P6 diesel engine, its six cylinders giving 65bhp. A five speed gearbox, with overdrive on the fifth gear was standard. Some operators fitted an Eaton two-speed rear axle.

The vehicle had just proved itself as reliable and economic and was finding favour with customers when World War 2 broke out and production was halted. The story of its success belongs to the postwar period.

Below:
Two Seddon 6ton lorries awaiting delivery to a Bradford customer who used the same fleet number for both vehicles!

Bottom:
Another Seddon 6tonner for a Yorkshire brewery.

Sentinel

The name Sentinel is synonymous with steam wagons, which were acclaimed throughout the world. The Scottish firm of Alley & McLellan of Polmadie, Glasgow, established the Sentinel in 1906, and moved to Shrewsbury in 1918. The vehicles were highly successful and until crippling legislation and taxes hit the steam road vehicles, they could be seen in many spheres of road haulage, for they were efficient, reliable, modern and virtually silent. A testimony to this is the fact that as late as 1950 — well over a decade since the last Sentinel steamer had been built for the UK market, the firm received an order for 250 six-wheelers from the Argentinian Naval Authority.

In the late 1930s the Sentinel steamers were fitted with such luxuries as electric speedometer drive, automatic cylinder lubrication, self-stoking boilers (filled through the cab roof), a power take-off for a dynamo, a small compressor for a tyre pump, plus — if required — tipping gear and steam heaters for keeping loads hot — such as tar, etc.

The range of models was large and improvements were continually made over the years; a conventional prop shaft having succeeded chain driven rear axles.

Sentinel also produced the High Speed Gas (HSG) producer plant, which they took over from Gilfords, but even with wartime petrol restrictions gas producer plant never became popular with operators. Sentinel also became interested in the internal combustion engine before the war.

Below:
A Super Sentinel 6/8ton four-wheeled steam lorry of 1925.

Right:
A type DG/6 supplied to Dunstable Portland Cement in 1932.

Below right:
Another six-wheeler of 1931.

Top:
This DG/6 model is fitted with 40in by 9in giant
pneumatic tyres and carries a 12ton payload.

Above:
The last steam design from Sentinel was the
S6T model. This example is fitted with a
three-way tipping body.

Shelvoke & Drewry

This firm was formed by a partnership of two ex-employees of the Lacre concern — Harry Shelvoke and J. S. Drewry — in 1923. Their initial production met with immediate success, for there was no competition for the ultra low loading vehicle they had designed. It was truly unique, with small 20in diameter wheels giving a 1ft 11in loading height, forward control with the driver sitting just ahead of the front axle, in a central position with tiller controls at either hand. The right hand tiller was for steering and the left for operating the vertically mounted epicyclic gearbox — three forward gears and one reverse.

The vehicles became popular with operators large and small, particularly with municipal authorities for use as refuse collecting vehicles where the low loading height was a considerable advantage. It was also economic in operation with a 14hp engine, a top speed of around 15mph, and also was highly manoeuvrable, with the added bonus that as the unladen weight was less than 2tons it came into a low taxation class.

From 1932 to 1939, Shelvoke & Drewry also produced the Latil tractors, under licence from the French manufacturers. It must also be mentioned that Shelvoke & Drewry also produced a few special vehicles with normal steering just prior to the war.

Below:
This 1934 S&D was given by Epsom & Ewell Borough Council in 1965 to the Worthing & District Vintage Vehicle Society for preservation. It is interesting to note that Worthing operated a fleet of S&D Tramocars prior to the war. *S. W. Stevens-Stratten*

Left:
An early S&D Freighter of 1926.

Bottom left:
This vehicle was supplied in 1927 for petrol delivery.

Bottom:
A rear loading dustcart of 1932.

Singer

Nowadays, the name Singer is normally associated with sewing machines, but the Singer Motors Ltd of Birmingham produced a large range of motor cars over many years. From 1929-1932 Singer also manufactured a series of commercial vehicles for payloads of 25cwt, 30cwt, 2ton and 45cwt capacity.

Although they do not appear to have had vast sales, Singer lorries incorporated several novel features, including electric starting, which in those days was considered to be a great refinement.

The engine for the 2ton model was a four-cylinder petrol unit of 3,053cc (90mm bore by 120mm stroke), which at 3,000rpm developed over 57bhp. The design of the overhead valve rockers reduced wear, while the lubrication system had no loose pipes. The chassis incorporated a Luvax foot-operated lubrication system supplying oil to the necessary parts, while the brakes were vacuum assisted. The engine was mounted on a three point suspension on a sub-frame insulated from the gearbox and clutch by rubber buffers. In the early 1930s this all added up to the most modern techniques.

Below:
The Singer Industrial Motors 2ton lorry of 1930 with all 'mod con'.

Right:
A 25cwt, six-cylinder, 160cu ft capacity, van of 1931. Finished in bright red with black wings, wheels, lamps and bonnet, plus gold lettering, it must have looked most attractive.

Bottom right:
A 45cwt chassis with a 500gal petrol tank body in 1931.

Star

The Star Engineering Company was formed in 1904, having previously been the Star Cycle Company from 1896 when it took over the engineering concern of Sherratt & Lisle. The company's works were at Frederick Street, Wolverhampton, and were thus easy prey for a take-over by Guy Motors in 1927 who changed the name to Star Motor Company.

Early Star vehicles were based on a motor car chassis, but from the 1920s some goods chassis were produced for payloads from 15cwt to 2ton. A four-cylinder side valve engine of 3,054cc was fitted to the smaller vehicles, while an overhead valve engine was used for larger models.

The Star Flyer lived up to its name, being a fast vehicle with a six-cylinder, 23.8hp engine, and carrying 3/4ton. The wheelbase was 14ft 2in and the chassis was occasionally used for small passenger carrying vehicles.

The company continued as a separate entity under the Guy management until it went into liquidation in 1931.

Below:
An articulated tractor unit of 1931, based on the 50cwt model with a 233.8hp (RAC rated) engine. The semi-trailer was built by Dyson.

Thornycroft

The first Thornycroft vehicle was a steam van built in 1896 at Chiswick, which proved so successful that many steam wagons were built. In 1902 the first petrol engined Thornycroft vehicle appeared from the new works at Basingstoke.

One of the turning points in the company's history occurred in 1912 when it introduced the J type 4½ton lorry powered by a 30hp side valve engine. This vehicle became a subsidy type and over 5,000 were supplied to the government during the 1914-18 war. The J type continued in production, with a larger 50hp engine until 1926.

The next success was in 1924 with the A1 chassis for 30cwt loads, and this and a modified chassis coded A2 for 2ton loads was the basis for a great variety of different bodies and many thousands were sold.

The PB forward control chassis came in 1928 and the QC six-wheeler in 1931 with a payload capacity of 12ton. From 1933 all the Thornycroft range were given names rather than letters — the Handy being the successor for the A1/2 models.

In 1933 Thornycroft produced the Taurus 6tonner with the engine placed ahead of the front axle, giving a snout effect, but allowing maximum load length for the given wheelbase. Another innovation around 1932 was the Stag six-wheeler using lightweight construction so that the unladen weight was under 7ton for a 12ton payload.

Other successful designs were the Sturdy for 6ton payloads introduced in 1936 and the Nippy 3tonner a year later, both these models being manufactured during World War 2 for essential civilian operation.

Thornycroft produced its first diesel engine in 1933 and thereafter these engines were available as an option for most of the range of models.

During World War 2 Thornycroft produced the Nubian four-wheel drive vehicle and Bren gun carriers. Thornycroft had considerable experience with cross-country vehicles, having supplied many pre-war army vehicles and others for the export market.

Below:
A 1910 box van supplied to the Leeds Industrial Co-operative Society.

Left:
Two Bulldog 2ton lorries supplied in 1932 to Blackpool Co-operative Society.

Above:
A 1919 J type 4ton lorry, the same as the 1913 subsidy type. This example has now been preserved. *Stevens-Stratten Collection*

Above right:
One of the first Thornycroft vehicles to be fitted with an oil engine in 1931.

Right:
A Manly 2ton lorry of 1934. The body length is 11ft.

Above:
The Dandy 3ton chassis is used for this 1,000cu ft van.

Top right:
The Nippy 3ton forward control chassis proved popular with many operators. This example has a 1,300cu ft van body for a well-known removals firm.

Right:
Three Handy 2ton forward control box vans supplied in 1934 to a well-known haulier.

Above:
The forward control Trusty 8ton lorry in this photograph is used for retail coal and coke sales.

Below:
Just prior to World War 2, Thornycroft announced its Sturdy 6ton chassis, which became popular and was used by the armed services.

Trojan

Words used to describe the Trojan included 'weird', 'ugly', 'unique' and 'just plain horrible'! Yet this vehicle, designed by L. H. Hounsfield, was produced by Leyland Motors in its Kingston-upon-Thames factory from 1924 and, at one time, production was at the rate of 85 per week. This association with Leyland lasted for four years, after which Trojan set up its own production plant at Purley Way, Croydon.

The original model, of 1924, carried a 5cwt payload, had thin solid tyres, chain drive, a two-speed epicyclic gearbox, the footbrake operated on the rear wheels and the handbrake on the transmission. The engine was a unique four-cylinder, two-stroke rated at 10hp (63.5mm by 120mm) and it had only seven moving parts!

Two years later a 7cwt model was produced, which could be fitted with pneumatic tyres and this lasted until 1933 when an improved model capable of taking a 10cwt load was introduced. It still used the same engine but the cylinders were now 63.5mm by 117.5mm. This model remained until 1937 when the 12cwt Senior was announced and this was fitted with Bendix-Cowdray brakes, but all the other features remained. One of the largest users of Trojan vans was Brooke Bond Tea, but many small retailers found them economical and easy to maintain.

Left:
Brooke Bonds Tea was among the largest users of Trojan vans. Here is a 1930-type van. *Pamlin Prints*

Below:
This 1934 Lightweight 7/10cwt van, featuring glass fibre reinforced plastics body panels has been preserved and is seen here on the HCVS Brighton run in 1965. *S. W. Stevens-Stratten*

Vulcan

The Vulcan Motor & Engineering Company Limited of Crossens, Southport, Lancashire was founded in 1904, producing a small number of vehicles. The company had many financial problems during the 1920s and these continued in the early 1930s. The receiver was called in, for the third time, in 1936 but on this occasion the company was unable to recover and was purchased by the trailer manufacturer, J. Brockhouse who only wanted the works and the land. Tilling Stevens therefore purchased the production rights and transferred the manufacture of Vulcan vehicles to its own works at Maidstone, Kent. At this time the range consisted of 2½ton,

3ton, and 5ton chassis which were continued with the option of different engines including a Vulcan one manufactured since 1932.

Tilling Stevens had designed a new 6ton forward control model, known as the 6VF, which would have been introduced at the 1939 Commercial Motor Show, had it not been cancelled due to World War 2. However, the company was able to produce this model for the civilian market from 1940 and with a choice of a petrol or diesel engine. Many operators took delivery of these vehicles as they were virtually the only new vehicles available. These vehicles produced in wartime austerity conditions had a wire mesh type of radiator grille.

Right:
A 1920 Vulcan model VSC 30cwt lorry which has now been preserved.

Below:
A 1934 3ton low loading refuse collector, fitted with hydraulic underslung tipping gear.

Top left:
A 50cwt van of 1930.

Centre left:
A 1938 model 5ton lorry.

Below:
The Vulcan 6VF model introduced in 1939 which was in limited production during the war years.

Some Smaller British Manufacturers

Belsize

Right:
Belsize fire appliances were built in conjunction with John Morris & Sons Ltd of Salford, and it appears that joint marketing arrangements were made. One of the earliest models was made in 1912 and production ceased in 1921. This 1912 model, now preserved, has a six-cylinder 14litre, 79hp engine. The wheelbase is 11ft. A Morris Ajax 60ft wheeled escape is carried. The appliance was converted to pneumatic from solid tyres in the late 1920s. It was used by the Southampton Fire Brigade and seen here on the HCVS Brighton run in 1965.
S. W. Stevens-Stratten

Crossley

Above:
Crossley Motors of Manchester was generally known as a bus builder, but in 1914 it made the RFC model ambulance and light van for the Royal Flying Corps. A Crossley four-cylinder engine of 4,531cc (101.6mm by 140mm) was fitted. The wheelbase is 11ft 4in long. This 1918-built restored van is participating in the HCVS London-Brighton run in 1974.
S. W. Stevens-Stratten

Crossley produced a few goods chassis in the 1920s and 1930s and this is a 4/6ton Beta model lorry of 1934 fitted with a four-cylinder 31.5hp engine.

Tilling-Stevens

Tilling-Stevens of Maidstone was a pioneer in the petrol-electric system of transmission and generally concentrated on the passenger chassis market. However, several chassis were used for commercial or goods bodies and a few goods chassis were produced in the late 1920s and 1930s. Tilling-Stevens produced searchlight lorries for the army during World War 2. This photograph shows a 4ton van of 1931.

Walker

Right:
Battery electric propulsion began as early as 1905, and in the early 1920s several makers were experimenting with this form of power. However, it was not until the petrol rationing of the 1940s and early 1950s that battery electric vehicles really became a practical proposition for operators and manufacturers alike. This is a 1919 Walker 1ton van (originally part American-built) which is now preserved.
S. W. Stevens-Stratten

Yorkshire

Above:
The Yorkshire Patent Steam Wagon Co of Leeds had manufactured steam lorries from the early days of 1900 on a small scale. This 1914 6ton steam wagon was new to the Colne Carrying Co of Colne, Lancashire. It was later sold to Bilston Blast Furnaces and then to a brickworks near Uttoxeter. This 6ton WE model is now preserved, and photographed at the Horsham Historic Vehicle Show in 1970.
S. W. Stevens-Stratten

British Lorries

1945-1992

Introduction

In updating this section, one is conscious not only of the changes which have been made to the design of heavy commercial vehicles, but also of the fact that there are now fewer British makes on the road. Two factors have caused this: first the great influx of vehicles produced by foreign manufacturers in direct competition with our own motor industry and, partly as an indirect result of this, the dearth of British manufacturers either through financial collapse or as the result of merger or take-over. In 1945, the beginning of this survey, there were 27 manufacturers; by 1982 this had been reduced to 11 and by 1992 to only eight. Of this eight only two, ERF and Dennis, are completely British.

There have been one or two additional firms which produced a few good vehicles during the period covered by this book — Argyle, Hillmaster, Proctor and Rowe — but their production was so small as to be virtually insignificant and all ceased after a period of only a couple of years or so.

Designs, as can be seen in the photographs that follow, have changed considerably during the 47-year period beginning with the continuation of the prewar models with small improvements. As the industry got into its stride in the civilian market, following experience with military vehicles and other wartime products, and with a steady flow of new materials, entirely new products began to appear. Vehicles became larger, more powerful and more refined, but the technical development also kept apace of the times, as did safety factors and the provision for the driver's comfort.

Nationalisation of the road haulage industry in 1947 saw the end of many interesting haulage operators and some distinctive liveries. Fortunately at that time many companies in the manufacturing and distributive trades operated their own fleets and thus there remained some variety of both makers and liveries.

When the British Railways network was cut back under Dr Beeching, road transport flourished and with the advent of the motorways the commercial vehicle came to reign supreme for the transport of goods from door-to-door, whether in the form of the small humble parcel or the bulk load. The range of operation has further been extended beyond the shores of the British Isles by the roll-on, roll-off ferries between the UK and the Continent and by our entry into the European Economic Community, both of which have served to give impetus to Continental work. Even when the railways are involved in the carriage of freight

in the form of container traffic, much of this starts and finishes its journey on the rear of a lorry.

It does not seem possible that 35 years ago a lorry weighing more than 3ton unladen was not permitted to exceed 20mph, but the Construction and Use regulations, which govern the design, size and weight of vehicles, have gradually been relaxed in accordance with modern requirements, although I feel sure that some operators would like to see them abandoned altogether!

As vehicles have become larger the media seem to refer to all commercial vehicles as 'Juggernauts' — a term which I feel is unjust or inappropriate. The dictionary states that a Juggernaut was a chariot taken in procession, when thousands contended the honour of dragging the vehicle, while many devotees threw themselves under its wheel to be crushed! It can also refer to a relentless human force which destroys blindly anything that comes in its way; hardly fair comment on drivers of heavy goods vehicles who are, generally speaking, among the finest on our roads today.

The Motor Show of 1990 had no commercial vehicle section and at the 1986 and 1988 shows some well-known manufacturers were not exhibiting. Such is the state of the industry today. Much of this has been laid on the recession, and this certainly has not helped, but the decline began well over a decade ago when the Continental manufacturers started to make inroads into the British market, offering improved and up-to-date vehicles with full service back-up. DAF, Mercedes, Renault, Scania and Volvo vehicles are now more common on the roads and motorways of the British Isles than our own British counterparts.

Of the British manufacturers left, many have lost their individuality with the use of components made by other concerns, and this particularly applies to the driver's cab. Many are using the designs of others, such as the units made by Motor Panels, and only the badge or a small variation in the radiator grille is different.

Driver's cab comfort has increased even further in the last decade, but again this is a standard which has been set by the continental manufacturers. Tilt cabs for easy access, which first appeared in 1962, are now normal for all heavy vehicles. With the greater use of the vehicle ferries across the Channel it is easy and economical for a vehicle to make regular trips from this country to all parts of Europe and beyond, so sleeper cabs have become standard for such vehicles. These can vary from a basic bunk behind the driver's seat (or above the normal roof level), to an elaborate set-up with cooker, small fridge, wash-basin, etc. Stereo radio/cassette players and air conditioning are now quite common, and with the addition of power-steering and good suspension, driving a 38ton truck is little greater effort than the family saloon.

The use of foreign engines is now widespread and few vehicles have the chassis builder's own engine. Again, it is a sad story as the famous Gardner diesels are now owned by Perkins, who are in turn controlled by the Varity Corporation of Canada. The American-owned Cummins company provides a large number of different engines fitted to British trucks, while other suppliers include Detroit Diesels and Caterpillar.

Continual changes in legislation, often instigated by the European Economic Community (generally known as the Common Market), have led to many alterations and new laws over the last few years affecting the construction and use of vehicles, drivers licences, emission of fumes, etc. The use of metric figures for measurement has almost abolished the old Imperial system. Measurements are now given in metres instead of feet, the litre is used to replace the gallon, and weight is expressed in kilogrammes or metric tonnes. One UK ton equals 1.0160 tonnes.

The use of articulated vehicles has risen dramatically in the past 20 years, for a weight of up to 38tonnes is now permitted. Semi-trailers are now fitted with two or three axles for such loads and operators who abhorred articulation in the past are now running such vehicles. Fairground operators and showmen are a case in point as it is now common to see tractor units and semi-trailers as fairground transport, often because the 'ride' is an integral part of the semi trailers, but this is not always the case.

It is apparent that there is now a great number of variations being offered in each model in respect of wheelbase lengths and engine options. Most models are now available in at least three or four different wheelbases, with a choice of engines, gearboxes and rear axles. The two-speed axle and 'splitter' gearbox are now quite common.

Bodywork has also changed for it has become more streamlined and many vehicles are now fitted with a roof-mounted wind deflector on the cab which makes for less wind resistance and consequently a better mileage per gallon. The curtain-sided body has become popular and this has a solid front, rear and roof but heavy quality

curtains at the sides. These can be drawn back for loading and unloading and then pulled forward and tied down to secure the load.

Liveries, too, have changed and it is now fashionable to have 'speed stripes' and chevrons adorning the vehicle, with no lettering, or at best the very minimum, often kept to the initials of the owner or operator. Many vehicles which appear to be owned by a company are in fact on contract hire and actually are owned by a transport or distribution specialist.

Once again, I wish to make it clear that the illustrations and text are not intended to give a complete list of all the models produced by the manufacturers concerned since 1945, but are designed to introduce the more common and popular types. The emphasis is on the heavier vehicles rather than on the car-derived vans and light trucks. All photographs, unless stated otherwise, are from the Ian Allan Library.

S. W. Stevens-Stratten, FRSA
Epsom
June 1992

AEC 1912-1979

The foundations of the Associated Equipment Company date back to 1906 and the Vanguard Bus Company, one of the many independent operators which joined the large London General Omnibus Company; thus AEC commenced to manufacture buses for the streets of London and from 1912 produced the immortal B type bus of World War 1 fame. A lorry chassis was produced in 1916 for use by the Forces, known as the Y type, which was also sold in the civilian market after hostilities were over. This was the beginning of commercial vehicle manufacture for AEC which continued to become one of the largest builders of buses and lorries in the UK.

The company moved from its original works at Walthamstow to Southall in Middlesex in 1927. At this time it had a brief merger with the British Daimler, beginning in 1926 and the name Associated Daimler (ADC) lasted for two years.

Below:

An AEC Mammoth Major eight-wheeler fitted with a six-cylinder, 9.6litre oil engine, capable of dealing with a 15ton payload. This design was outwardly little changed since it was first introduced in 1933. The vehicle was supplied to a well-known transport contractor in the early 1950s.

During the 1920s AEC was producing vehicles with payloads of 6ton to 13½ton, each model bearing a name such as Mercury, Majestic, Mammoth Major and Mandator, many of these names being carried on the range until lorry production ceased.

During World War 2 production was switched to War Department requirements and AEC produced 9,620 Matador 4x4 medium artillery tractors, 514 Marshall six-wheel 2,500gal refuelling tankers for the RAF, 192 Marshall six-wheel vehicles, many of which had a Coles Crane mounted, 185 similar vehicles for mobile oxygen plants, 629 armoured cars plus diesel engines for the Valentine tank and many other items vital to the services and the country generally.

The return to civilian production in 1948 saw the range consisting of the Matador and Monarch, both four-wheel vehicles for a 12ton gross weight, but with the former capable of hauling a trailer; the Mammoth Major six-wheeler for 19ton gross and the eight-wheeled version with the same name capable of a 22ton gross weight.

AEC took over the old established firm of Maudslay Motor Co Ltd of Alcester (near Coventry) in 1948, also Crossley Motors Ltd of Manchester. Soon after there was change of name to Associated Commercial Vehicles Ltd, but the

initials AEC were kept on the vehicles. In 1949 ACV acquired the body-building firms of Park Royal Vehicles and its subsidiary Charles H. Roe of Leeds but, as both were engaged on bodies for passenger vehicles, it had little effect on commercial vehicle production.

In 1953 an older name was revived — the Mercury — for an 8ton payload with a cruising speed of 40mph. A Park Royal-designed cab was later fitted and appeared on all models about this time.

With large development in the building of motorways and civil engineering generally, AEC entered the earth-moving field in 1957 and produced a large six-wheel, 10cu yd Dumptruck, later building several sizes including an 18cu yd four-axle model. Production of these vehicles under the AEC label ceased around 1967.

Another acquisition was made in 1961 when Transport Equipment (Thornycroft) was absorbed into the ACV empire and production of the normal range of commercial vehicles under that name ceased, although the specialised vehicles such as airport fire-fighting tenders and the Mighty Antars for oilfield and off-the-road work continued.

In August 1962 Associated Commercial Vehicles merged with Leyland Motors and although the AEC range continued it slowly lost its identity, the first outward sign being the adoption of the Leyland Ergomatic cab in 1964 and production was gradually rationalised to avoid undue competition. Finally the name AEC disappeared from commercial vehicles in 1977 (although it continued on buses and coaches for another 18 months or so); the Leyland Marathon being made at Southall until the factory finally closed its gates in 1979.

It is tragic that AEC, founded in 1912 and known throughout the World as 'Builders of London Buses' is no longer in existence, being the victim of Leyland takeover.

Above:
The Mercury 8ton gcw chassis was introduced in 1953 and less than a year later was carrying the redesigned cab shown here, which was quickly fitted on all AEC models. In 1955 the Mercury was uprated for a 10ton payload and was available with four different wheelbases and a choice of two sizes of engine.

Below:
This Mandator tractor and semi-trailer could carry a payload of 32ton and this 1965 example is in the grey and yellow livery of Ferrymasters whose vehicles traverse Europe.

Above:

This Marshall six-wheel chassis has an 11cu yd tipper body. It was supplied to a South London contractor during the 1960s. Note the articulation of the rear bogie and the one-piece windscreen.

Right:

The Majestic was in effect a lengthened Mandator having a 19ft wheelbase and twin-steering front axles for a 10-11ton payload.

Above:
The London Brick Company had a large fleet of Mammoth Majors for the carriage of loose bricks. Nowadays most of their loads are on pallets.

Below:
The Marshall rigid six was available as a 6x2 or 6x4, with a choice of three different wheelbases and six- or 12-speed overdrive gearbox. This 1968 model was fitted with an AEC AV505 diesel engine developing 154bhp. The vehicle has the Leyland-designed Ergomatic cab.

Above:
**A Mandator prime mover for 32ton gcw. This
was fitted with a V8 engine giving 272bhp. Six-
or 10-speed semi-automatic transmission
could be offered as alternatives.**

Left:
**One of the range of
dumptrucks which AEC
built. This one has a 5cu
yd capacity and is
working on an opencast
site where it could take
an average payload of
28ton.**

Albion 1901-1972

The Albion Motor Car Co Ltd was formed at Scotstoun, near Glasgow in 1901 and a year later produced its first commercial vehicle which was really a motor car with a body adapted for the carriage of goods. By 1910 it had developed the A10-model truck which had a carrying capacity of 3ton, powered by a 32hp engine, and the model remained in production for 16 years giving the firm much publicity and establishing the reliability and ruggedness of the Scottish product with the slogan 'Sure as the Sunrise'.

During World War 1 the company manufactured thousands of subsidy-type lorries for the War Department, continuing production on an even larger scale when peace returned. In 1931 the word 'Car' was dropped from the company name. The small firm of Halley, which manufactured vehicles in a small plant at Yoker, near Scotstoun, was absorbed in 1935.

Wartime production of Albions consisted of 3ton 4x4 trucks and the 10ton 6x4 bonneted tractor for tank transporters. Production of civilian types recommenced in 1947 with a range of six chassis — the CX7, an eight-wheeler for a 14½ton payload; the CX5 a six-wheeler for 12ton payload; the CX1 and CX3, 7ton and 6½ton four wheelers, and two lighter models — the FT3 4-5ton and AZ5 for 1½ton loads. Improved versions and other models followed at intervals during the next few years, but in 1951 the company was acquired by Leyland Motors and although production continued the Leyland influence gradually made itself felt. This was noticeable in the cab design and from 1968 the outward appearance of the old Albion features had virtually disappeared.

In 1955 Albion introduced the Claymore a 4/5ton chassis with an underfloor engine — a Leyland 0.300 diesel unit. As this was mounted amidships it enabled the cab to be built forward of the front axle, thus giving a good turning circle with the maximum body length for the size of the vehicle — an ideal combination for local delivery and collection work. The Caledonian 16½ton payload rigid-eight was introduced in 1958 and was generally a competitor to the Leyland Octopus.

By 1972 the name Albion had disappeared, to be replaced by Leyland, although the now-closed plant at Scotstoun continued to produce many of the smaller vehicles in the Leyland range — the Redline in particular.

Below:
A 6½ton Albion which although delivered to its operator in 1951 was still the same basic design as prewar vehicles. It was used for the distribution of bottled beers and mineral waters.

Above:

A Super Reiver 6x4 chassis fitted with light weight tipping body for the carriage of bulk grain.

Centre right:

Carrying a special body for the transport of pigeons, this Chieftain Super Six was fitted with the Leyland 400 engine. The body was of fibreglass while the whole of the roof was translucent, admitting natural light. The chassis had been extended by 5ft to give an overall length of 34ft.

Bottom right:

A Clydesdale, 1,750gal milk tanker, one of a very large number purchased for the bulk collection of milk from farms. The electric motor for the pump was driven by high capacity batteries which were charged by the vehicle's engine during normal running.

Above:
The Claymore was popular for suburban collection and delivery work. This is a 4ton model with a 72hp horizontal diesel engine; the body has a capacity of 644cu ft.

Below:
This 20ton Reiver bulk grain carrier was delivered in 1968. It had full pneumatic discharging equipment and the dimensions of the body were 7ft 8in wide, 4ft 10in deep and 21ft long which with the boxed headboard gave a capacity of 700cu ft. The vehicle has the Leyland type Ergomatic cab.

Above:
A Super Clydesdale tractor and semi-trailer which had a plated gtw of 22ton for UK operation.

Below:
At the Scottish Motor Show in 1957 this Caledonian eight-wheeled chassis was fitted with a 3,900gal tank for the transport of transformer oil. Note the Leyland influence in the cab design.

Atkinson 1916-1970

Edward Atkinson, the founder of the firm was an engineer of some repute and from 1907 became an expert in repairing and servicing steam vehicles as well as being an agent for Alley and McLellan, the forerunner of Sentinel. In 1916 he designed and built his own steam wagon — a 6ton four-wheeler and in the early 1920s was manufacturing about three wagons a week with a staff of nearly 150. However, the economic depression of the late 1920s caused the company to flounder and it was reconstituted as Atkinson Lorries Ltd in 1933 for the production of diesel-powered vehicles using the Gardner engine. Production was small and financial difficulties were ever present. Luckily, wartime contracts for 160 six-wheel and 100 eight-wheel vehicles saved the company and after the cessation of hostilities it was able to relaunch its range of four-, six- and eight-wheeled vehicles, the design of which remained basically unaltered until 1953, when the cabs were redesigned with the familiar bow front.

In 1957 heavier vehicles were marketed with an eye to cross-country and oil-field operations, and the Omega bonneted 6x6 100ton vehicles with Rolls-Royce engines were produced. In 1958 fibre glass cabs which incorporated a wrap-round windscreen were fitted to most of the range.

During the early 1960s Atkinson began manufacturing the Black Knight range of four-, six- and eight-wheeled freight vehicles, the Gold Knight chassis for tippers and concrete mixers (short wheelbase) and the Silver Knight tractor units. During 1968 some Atkinson vehicles were produced with a German Krupp-manufactured cab on a Silver Knight chassis for the European market, but the UK production consisted of the Borderer 4x2 tractor unit, the Searcher rigid-six and the Defender rigid-eight, plus the Omega bonneted 100ton heavy tractor. In 1966 the Viewline cab was introduced, but it was not very popular with operators and was dropped a few years later.

Below:
An Atkinson 15ton payload eight-wheeler supplied in 1954 and having the same external appearance as vehicles supplied prior to 1939. Painted dark green with yellow lettering it had a smart and dignified appearance.

In 1970 Atkinson was finally acquired by Seddon, but production continued and in 1972 the Leader rear-steering tractor unit was launched along with a large 8x4 tipping lorry chassis using the Gardner 150 engine, which was also fitted in some other trucks of larger size. During the early 1970s the Searcher 6x4 chassis proved popular for cement mixers. The emphasis, however, was on tractor units, the Venturer 6x4 and the Borderer 4x2 chassis being offered with a choice of engines, although usually those by Gardner or Cummins were fitted.

Seddon Atkinson (qv) was taken over by International Harvester of America in 1974, that firm already having a European interest when it acquired a holding in the Dutch DAF concern.

Vehicles are now marketed as Seddon Atkinson and the 400-series is a range of 12 models—six tractors, a 30½ ton and 32ton gcw (with Gardner, Rolls-Royce or Cummins engines); a 30½ton and 32ton gtw four-wheeler capable of towing a trailer; a 24ton gvw rigid-six and a 30 ton rigid-eight, (Gardner or Cummins engines for all the last three types). Sleeper cabs can be provided on all chassis. There is also the 200-series of 16ton rigid-fours with choice of three wheelbase lengths all of which have the International engine fitted. Recently the Atkinson 'Big A' motif has been reintroduced on the larger members of the Seddon Atkinson range.

Below:

A Silver Knight tractor unit operated by a well known Scottish haulier. The 20ton payload unit was fitted with a Rolls-Royce diesel engine.

Left:
New in 1960 this Silver Knight eight-wheeler and trailer could carry a 22ton payload at a steady 52mph on motorways, The glass fibre cab is above a Gardner 6LX engine developing 150bhp transmitting its power through a ZF six-speed gearbox.

Below:
Model T746X a 7½-8ton tractor of 1960 coupled to a York Freightmaster tandem-axle box van lightweight semi-trailer. It was used for the transport of crated beer.

Above:

One of 17 such vehicles built in 1963 especially for gritting and salting the motorways in inclement weather.

Below:

An Atkinson tractor on heavy haulage duties. The 43ton load, which was 93ft long was being taken from Glasgow to Treforest.

Austin 1910-1968

The first commercial vehicles made by Austin were 15cwt models based on a car chassis but in 1913 a 3ton truck developing 29hp from its four-cylinder engine was produced. It was a forward-control vehicle and possibly far in advance of its time. Apart from a few odd models in the early 1920s and light delivery vans on car chassis, the Austin Motor Co did not compete in the commercial field until 1938/39 when it commenced manufacture of a range of 30cwt, 50cwt, 2-3ton and up to 5ton vehicles. The heavier models had an appearance not unlike that of their competitors, Bedford, so they became known as the 'Birmingham Bedfords'.

During the last war Austin produced its K2 vehicles in large numbers for use as Army ambulances and also for emergency fire tenders which towed a trailer pump. Austin also produced the K3 4x2 3ton general service lorry, the K6 6x4 chassis used as aircraft refuellers etc and the K5, the 4x4 general duty lorries which soon became nicknamed 'screamers' on account of the noise emitted from the four-wheel drive mechanism and gearbox.

After the war Austin came into its own and a vast number of K2 3ton chassis were produced together with the K4 five-tonner plus the unique three-way forward-control van (type K8) which had a payload of 25cwt with a 2 litre petrol engine

(an alternative Perkins diesel engine was offered later). Production of this type continued until 1954.

In 1952 Austin and Morris merged to form the British Motor Corporation and some unification of the two ranges began. Identical vehicles could be seen with the badge of either Austin or Morris on their radiators, although as a rough guide Austin appeared on normal-control and Morris on forward-control vehicles. See also the chapter on BMC.

Below:

An Austin 2ton van of 1957 operated by British Road Services (Parcels) Ltd. The bodies incorporated alloy panels, the floor was of wood, and the one-piece roof was translucent plastic.

Above:
A 4ton forward-control chassis with a Bonallack light alloy Luton-type box body. The vehicle was 21ft long and 9ft 8in high.

Below:
A modified 25cwt three-way van utilised by Austin for a tour of UK dealers.

Top:
A type FJ 18ton gtw prime mover powered by a 120bhp 5.7litre BMC underfloor diesel engine and five-speed direct-drive gearbox to BMC two-speed axle. The semi-trailers were built by Carrimore and delivered in 1965.

Above:
A one-ton Austin van with body capacity of 235cu ft. It was available with petrol or diesel engine. The 1½ton version had a capacity of 275cu ft but was virtually the same with 8ft 4½in wheelbase, an overall length of 14ft 7¼in and height of 7ft 8½in.

Above:

This 3ton parcels van was designed in 1958 by BMC and BRS, the latter using many hundreds of the type. Known as 'Noddy Vans' the chassis was modified with drivers' foot controls moved back 11in and steering altered accordingly to enable the driver to enter and leave his seat without climbing over the wheelarch. The body had a 600cu ft capacity and a floor height of only 3ft 3in. The cab was fitted with a sliding door and the driver could walk through to the rear.

Below left:

Driver's cab of the type VA 'Noddy Van' showing access to the walk-through cab.

Below:

Introduced in the late 1960s the FF series was for a 5ton payload, but was later uprated. Engine was either a BMC petrol or diesel developing 90 or 105bhp.

Bedford 1931-1992

The Vauxhall Iron Works produced marine engines and from 1902 became increasingly involved in the new petrol-engined cars. A move to Luton and a change to complete car production proved successful and in the late-1920s the business was acquired by the American giant, General Motors. This company had been struggling to import its Chevrolet trucks into Great Britain, so this acquisition proved to be a turning point; the Chevrolets were redesigned for the British market in 1931 and vehicles were produced at the Vauxhall plant at Luton under the name Bedford. The 2ton lorry with 26hp six-cylinder petrol engine was an immediate success and by 1939 a range of vehicles from 12cwt to 5ton was available.

In 1938 a redesigned radiator grille with rounded front was introduced which became the hallmark for many years, although during the war years a civilian version of the military OY-series, designated the OW-series, appeared with a straight utility bonnet and radiator grille.

Production for the War Department totalled some 250,000 trucks the most numerous being the 15cwt (pneumonia wagon), the 3ton 4x2 GS truck and the forward-control 4x4 QL model.

Manufacture for the civilian market was resumed in 1947 with the same prewar models and in 1950 the first of the Big Bedfords appeared — the 7ton S-type semi-forward control with a new cab and differing wheelbases; there was also a short wheelbase 8ton tractor unit.

In 1960 a radical new design appeared, the now famous TK range with the engine mounted longitudinally immediately behind the drivers cab, thus giving full forward control. New 8cwt vans using many components from the Vauxhall Viva cars were made in 1964. Two years later the KM range for up to 24ton gvw were produced taking Bedford into the heavy market, and this was increased for 32ton gcw when tractor units were introduced in 1972.

In 1976 the production of the TJ bonneted range which started in 1962 ceased. This was superseded by the JM range and in 1978 the TK 4x2 and 6x2 range was extended from 5½ton to 16ton gvw. Changes again took place in 1980 when the TK range was joined by the tilt-cab TL range, which brings Bedford in the forefront of modern design.

In the early 1980s Bedford was still one of the leading manufacturers of commercial vehicles and their old slogan of 'You See Them Everywhere' still held good. An internal change of ownership occurred at the end of 1983 when control passed to General Motors' Worldwide Truck & Bus Group in Pontiac, Michigan, but apart from the more common use of the Detroit diesel little outward change was apparent. However, the first stages of the recession were beginning to hit the motor industry generally and in 1985 there were voluntary redundancies and it was announced that

Below:
A 5ton Bedford van of the 1950s. This vehicle operated by a well-known toy firm was fitted with a Pallet-Jekta telescopic floor for palletised loading.

Bedford had made a trading loss of approximately £11 million for the year. The total loss at that time was put at about £73 million. Talks were in progress with British Leyland regarding a take-over or a merger and short-time working came into effect at the Luton and Dunstable plants.

In order to keep a place in the market Bedford began the production of two Japanese designed light vans — the Rascal based on the Suzuki Super Carry and the Midi based on the Isuzu vehicle. These, however, did not provide the salvation that was expected and other Bedford models were slowly discontinued until, in 1986, a decision was made to pull out of the heavy vehicle market apart from military vehicles (mainly the TN 6x6 type).

In 1987 Bedford was sold to a British concern, AWD Ltd (All Wheel Drive), who acquired the Dunstable plant and the rights to the Bedford truck and bus range which had been discontinued in 1986. The intention was to market some of the Bedford TL and TM range but concentrating on military contracts and four- and six-wheel drive vehicles. However, on 4 June 1992 it was announced that AWD was in the hands of the receivers.

Above left:
Introduced in 1952 the CA 10/12cwt van was an immediate success and produced for over two decades. It was powered by a 1594cc petrol engine as used in the Vauxhall Wyvern car.

Below left:
In the early 50s when the Bedford range was redesigned some models were then known as the 'Big Bedford'. This S-type tractor unit used by a London grocers was fitted with a Adrolic anti-jack knife stabiliser.

Above:
A 1957 Big Bedford 6cu yd tipper.

Right:
In 1959 the normal-control range was redesigned. Here is a 6ton tipper traversing some rough terrain.

Above:
The TK range from 2ton to 12ton tractor units. This is a 1965 model of a 2ton chassis with Hawson box van body for collection and delivery work.

Below:
A 2,600gal tanker on a 13ft 2in wheelbase KM tipper chassis. The tank has five compartments and the roller-shutter locker on the nearside houses delivery hoses etc.

Top left:
The CF series of vans was introduced for the 1970s and bears a close resemblance to the American General Motors vehicle. It is available for 18, 22, 35 and 35cwt loads. This is a one-ton model powered by a 1.8litre petrol engine used by the Scottish Gas Board.

Centre left:
A 1982 model of the CF chassis. This CF350D small truck is fitted with an aluminium box body and is on contract hire to W. H. Smith from Toller Hire.

Below:
Designed for a maximum weight of 38ton the TM3800 is the 'Big Bedford' of the 1980s. Fitted with a sleeper cab, the TM can be fitted with Bedford or Cummins engines.

Above:
The Bedford TM2600 six-wheel rigid is rated at 26tonnes gvw, with a Bedford 8.2litre diesel developing 208bhp at 2,500rpm. This example for Northern Dairies has been 'stretched' by adding an extra 64in to the wheelbase and an additional 35in to the rear overhang. *VRPL*

Below:
The 1983 middleweight TL models have Bedford turbocharged engines as standard, plus tilt cabs, and replaced the earlier TK range. This 12ft 4in tipper is one of five wheelbase options. *VRPL*

Above:
A 1986 model TL2440 24tonne 6x4 tipper engaged on quarry work. *VRPL*

Left:
Bedford started production of a battery-electric version of the CF van in 1984 for the lighter payload market. This is a prototype with an ice-cream Luton-type body by Robin Hood Vehicle Builders of Southampton. *VRPL*

156

Left:
Bodywork for this 1986 CF2/350 ambulance was undertaken by Wadham Stringer of Waterlooville in Hampshire. The wheelbase is 10ft 6in and petrol or diesel engines can be fitted. *VRPL*

Top:
Throughout the 1980s the Bedford CF range was produced. This 230D model for a one ton payload is fitted with a General Motors four-cylinder diesel engine. *VRPL*

Above:
Although not strictly within the sphere of this book this illustrates a 1986 model of the Bedford Rascal. This was a model based on the Japanese Suzuki Super Carry, with a payload capacity of 650kg (12.75cwt) and a wheelbase of 1.84m (approximately 5ft 11in). These are still being marketed under the Vauxhall Motors banner since the demise of Bedford. *VRPL*

BMC 1952-1970

BMC — British Motor Corporation — was founded in 1952 following the merger of Austin and Morris (whose entries should be consulted) and these two concerns began to integrate their designs, although for the first four years both continued to market their own models. The BMC letters appeared on some models from 1956, notably the 7ton forward-control trucks (which also had the Austin or Morris badge), then when the British Motor Corporation merged with Leyland in 1968 the BMC name was used for two years but was dropped from 1970 when the larger vehicles became Leyland and the small vans and pick-up trucks reverted to Austin Morris. More recently this latter sector of the British Leyland empire became known as Freight Rover (qv).

Below:

The EA type van was a 30cwt nominal payload vehicle with walk-through cab and underfloor engine (70bhp petrol or 66bhp diesel) and was available in two body lengths.

The Mastiff 16ton rigid four-wheeler powered by a Perkins V8 engine. The vehicle has a tilt cab and was one of the largest to carry the BMC badge. It was later marketed as Leyland.

Bristol 1952-1964

The Bristol Tramways & Carriage Company was founded in 1887 and ran its first motorbus in the Bristol area in 1906. It manufactured its own vehicles from 1908, many being also sold to outside operators. Later the company was acquired by the Thomas Tiling Group of bus operators, which was Nationalised in 1947, passing into the control of the British Transport Commission (BTC). As a result of this Bristol only produced passenger vehicles for the Nationalised bus companies.

In 1952 Bristol produced its first goods vehicle chassis for the Road Haulage Executive, later to be renamed British Road Services, the goods haulage side of the BTC.

The first goods vehicles were rigid eight-wheelers with a maximum carrying capacity of 22ton (the heaviest permitted at that time). Powered by the Leyland 0.600 diesel engine of 125bhp they used gearboxes, transmission and other parts of Bristol manufacture. Later the cab was redesigned and a total of 517 rigid units were produced.

An articulated prime mover was introduced as model HA6L with Leyland 0.600 engine and this was also used by British Road Services.

Production of all goods vehicles ceased in 1964 (buses continuing) and Bristol was later denationalised when British Leyland took a substantial shareholding. Later, a new connection with the nationalised passenger sector was made, when Bristol became part of Bus Manufacturers (Holdings) Ltd, a joint undertaking of British Leyland and the National Bus Company. It is worth noting that this Bristol company had no connection with motor cars of the same name, as that was a subsidiary of Bristol Aircraft.

Below:
One of the earlier Bristol rigid-eights fitted with the Leyland 0.600 9.8litre engine.

Above:
A Bristol tractor unit and semi-trailer for BRS, with an overall length of 34ft 6½in.

Below:
A tractor unit positioning a Roadrailer at a railhead. The road wheels are about to be raised and the rail wheels lowered for coupling to the trailer at the rear to form the train.

Commer 1907-1976

Commercial Cars Ltd was founded in 1907 and had a chequered career. It was moderately successful in its earlier days, then financial troubles overtook the firm and it was taken over by Humber Cars in 1926, which was itself acquired by the Rootes Group in 1928. The name was abbreviated to Commer and the 1930s proved successful. Just prior to the war it introduced the Superpoise range of popular and well-designed vehicles.

The Commer contribution to the war effort produced over 20,000 vehicles for the three services, including the tractor units for the 60ft long 'Queen Mary' semi-trailers used by the RAF for the carriage of aircraft fuselages and wings.

Resuming production of the normal-control Superpoise after the war it added a Commer-Hands 6-8ton tractor and semi-trailer unit, and the normal-control 25cwt van, which shortly afterwards became available as forward-control model. In 1948 a redesigned range was put on the market with underfloor engines for 5ton and 7ton payloads, both being full forward-control. A new two-stroke diesel engine was marketed in 1953 having two horizontally-opposed pistons in each of the three cylinders. This engine was fitted to certain of the range, but alternative Perkins diesel engines of conventional design were also offered. The Superpoise range was extended in 1955 with 2-5ton vehicles with a six-cylinder diesel engine while the 15cwt vans had a four-cylinder engine.

A delivery van of exceptional merit was introduced in 1961 for 1½-3ton payloads; this was the Walk-thru van with semi-forward control and it remained in production long after the name was dropped.

Below:
A 5ton Superpoise tipper with 4cu yd body capacity. This model was fitted with a Perkins P6 diesel engine. There is little difference to cab and bonnet design from the prewar model.

A range of forward-control medium-weight vehicles appeared in 1963 later to be superseded by the V range. In 1966 Commer entered the heavier market with a 16ton gcw chassis and cab, having produced the Maxiload tractor unit for 12ton lorries in 1962.

In 1964, the American giant Chrysler got a foot into the Rootes empire, gaining complete control in 1973. Chrysler, which already owned Dodge in the USA and which firm had made trucks in the UK since 1933 (see separate chapter) somewhat naturally decided to market all the Commer range as Dodge, thus the old established name of Commer disappeared from 1976 except for a few municipal vehicles which also appeared under the Karrier name. These changes had already partly been put into practice when the Commando models were marketed as Karrier in 1974.

In 1978 the French Peugeot-Citroen Group purchased the Chrysler European interest.

Above right:
A Commer 1¼ton forward-control van of 1956 with a distinct Karrier-style front end.

Right:
A 12ton tractor unit fitted with TS3 engine coupled to a 2,000gal tanker delivered in 1955.

Left:
The new Superpoise normal control ¾ton chassis introduced in 1956.

Right:
One of the last Commer designs — an 8ton platform lorry of 1962. The wheelbase was 15ft 7in.

Above:
The well known Walk-thru van. This is the 1½ton model (the 2ton has twin rear wheels, but is otherwise the same). It has a Rootes diesel engine developing 56bhp. Overall length 17ft 2in, width 6ft 9¼in, height 5ft 9⅝in and wheelbase 10ft 3in. The price complete in 1961 was £952.

Dennis 1904-To date

John Dennis commenced building cycles in 1885 and later bought his younger brother Raymond into the rapidly expanding business. It was a simple step from cycles to the early motorcycles (called Speed Kings) and thus on to motorcars. Dennis Brothers of Guildford produced its first commercial vehicle in 1904 and had two 14hp two-cylinder models and 20, 24 and 28hp four-cylinder vehicles also available two years later. Fire engine production actually started as early as 1908 and a year earlier it had produced a worm-drive 5ton lorry.

The War Department 3½ton subsidy lorry of 1913 was produced in large numbers and following these the 2½ton chassis was used for municipal vehicles such as refuse collectors, gully emptiers, cesspool emptiers, etc.

By 1918, Dennis had acquired the well known Coventry engine manufacturer, White and Poppe, but did not enter the heavy market in the 1920s; even in the 1930s it was concentrating on the 2ton-6ton range with the exception of the six-wheeled 12-tonner introduced in 1931. In 1933 Dennis produced its popular Ace models which became known as 'Flying Pigs' because of the Protruding snout-like bonnet ahead of the front axle. A heavier vehicle, called the Max, appeared in 1937 having a payload of 6-7ton and full forward control.

Wartime production was large numbers of trailer fire pumps and various vehicles for the services.

Production resumed in 1946 with the Max and the Pax 5ton. Also a new 12ton six-wheeled chassis called the Jubilant which had a five-speed

gearbox and a 7.6litre engine later enlarged to 8litre. This later engine also powered the Centaur forward-control 6-7ton rigid lorry introduced in 1948 and the 12ton Horla tractor unit.

In 1954 Dennis produced a new design of 3ton payload van with an underfloor engine, called the Stork, but it does not appear to have been very popular. The Max was replaced by the Hefty in 1957 and also the Centaur by the Condor for 7ton payloads. The heavy market from 1964 was supplied with the Maxim — a four-wheel rigid 16ton and a six-wheel 22ton gvw vehicle of similar type but again this does not appear to have been very successful. However throughout this period the production of fire appliances and municipal refuse collectors using the Paxit compressing system was considerable.

At a time when Dennis was experiencing the closure of its bus building activities and with less sales of commercial vehicles it was acquired by the Hestair Group which injected capital into the organisation.

During the mid-to late-1970s the emphasis was on the establishment of a completely new passenger range, but production of refuse collectors, fire appliances and other municipal/specialist vehicles continued, with a very limited production of general haulage vehicles to special order. However in 1979 the Delta 16ton freight chassis for tipper and general haulage applications was revitalised with a new metal cab and went into full-scale production, albeit in smaller quantities than those of other manufacturers. Like the then Dennis range it was available with a wide range of engine/gearbox options.

In the last decade Dennis has established itself as one of the leading British bus and coach manufacturers, as well as continuing to supply fire appliances and municipal vehicles to special order.

The old plant at Guildford has given way to a brand new factory a couple of miles away, which now produces all the chassis, while the Ogle-designed cabs for the commercials are produced at the Eagle factory at Warwick, where the bodywork for the refuse collecting vehicles is also manufactured. The bodywork for fire appliances is sub-contracted.

There is only one commercial vehicle chassis now produced and this is the Delta for a payload of 16ton with a choice of Perkins or Gardner engines, although some other makes can be fitted. The Delta has been in production since 1980 with few modifications.

Left:
A normal control Pax 5ton vehicle supplied in 1945, continuing the prewar design.

Top left:
Few examples of the Centaur tractor were built. This one dates from 1954 and was fitted with a 5½litre engine.

Centre left:
A 1958 forward control Pax II fitted with a petrol engine. It had a loading height of only 3ft 3in.

Below:
Ten years on from the previous illustration — a Pax V chassis and cab for a 15ton gvw.

Above:
A Pax II model of 1961 vintage for carrying a non-vintage beverage!

Left:
This 3ton underfloor-engined Stork had a light alloy body with a cubic capacity of 950ft. It was delivered in 1954.

Above:
This Pax fitted with a Perkins P6 oil engine, supplied in 1957, was notable for its modern cab design.

Below:
A Dennis model RS135 standard water tender/ladder appliance supplied to the Devon Fire & Rescue Service in October 1988. The equipment specification is to the requirements of the customer. Anti-skid brakes by Girling are now standard equipment. *Girling*

Above:
Not unlike the Stork is this Heron removals van of 1960.

Dodge 1922-1987

The American company Dodge Brothers was assembling its imported parts in Britain in 1922 and in 1933 commenced manufacture of British chassis, but with American engines and gearboxes, at its works at Kew with its associated company, Chrysler. In the mid-1930s it concentrated on production of a semi-forward-control design of lorries and achieved some success with a 4-5ton short-wheelbase tipper. There was also a 30cwt van and a 2ton lorry.

After the war production recommenced at Kew with a range from 2ton to 6ton with a cab similar to that fitted to the Leyland Comet and in 1957 a 7ton chassis was offered with a Perkins R6 engine. An entirely new range made its appearance in 1956/57, of normal-control outline, and two years later a range of forward-control vehicles extended the range to 22ton gvw. These vehicles used proprietary parts such as Perkins engines and Motor Panels cabs as used on some Leyland and Albion models.

When Chrysler finally gained control of the Commer concern in 1973 there was much changing of badges and in 1976 the Dodge badge appeared on Commer-designed vehicles from the 1¼ton Spacevan to the 7-12ton Commando.

The Kew plant closed in 1967 and all production was switched to the Commer/Karrier plant at Dunstable. Further changes still took place and in 1980 the K series with tilt cabs were withdrawn.

By 1980, however, Chrysler, having control of Dodge (also Commer and Karrier badged as Dodge since c1976), found that it had a loss making concern on its hands and in 1978 sold its European business to Peugeot, who were subsequently taken over by the Renault organisation in 1981.

In 1982 the Dodge range consisted of the 300 series and the 100 series Commando ranges, which continued to flow from the Dunstable plant, but these models had an increasing percentage of foreign-sourced parts. The 300 series were imported from Spain and this ceased soon after the Renault take-over, although of course the models could be seen on the roads for many years afterwards.

The 100 Commando series ranged from 7.6 to 26ton tractive units and was first introduced in 1973. Although modified in 1981, the series was phased out from 1986 to be replaced by Renault models.

The original Commer-designed Walk-thru van of 1961, later badged as Dodge, was discontinued in 1978 and replaced by the 50 series for capacities from 3.5ton to 7.5ton.

By 1987 the name Dodge had little connection with British manufactured vehicles.

Below:
A Dodge 2/3ton van supplied in 1948 to the same design as prewar models.

Top:
With a cab similar to some Ford models, this Dodge tractor unit had a Perkins engine and was delivered to its operator in 1955.

Above:
A 3ton van of 1953. Fitted with a 114bhp petrol engine it has a light alloy body which was finished in yellow and blue. The bonnet and radiator have a similarity with the Leyland Comet.

Right:
A forward-control 5ton van of 1958. The wheelbase was 13ft 7in and the body had a capacity of 1,200cu ft. It had a glass fibre reinforced plastic roof.

Top:
The Dodge Walk-thru van was based on the original Commer design. The model was available in two wheelbases and a choice of three engines and from 1¼ to 3ton payload. This model has a Perkins diesel engine and a wheelbase of 10ft 3in.

Above:
A 1967 13ton tilt cab tipper with a Perkins 120bhp diesel engine and a wheelbase of 10ft 8in. This is one of the Dodge 500 series of vehicles.

Above:
A 100 series Commando lightweight box van with the Hi-Line tilt cab. Models in this range cater for 4½-12ton payloads with choice of Perkins diesel or Chrysler V8 petrol engines.

Below:
The 300 series 32ton tractor. Fitted with a Chrysler 11.9litre turbocharged diesel engine and a nine-speed gearbox.

The Dodge 50 series replaced the old Walk-thru vans, but were also available as a chassis/cab. The cab is a design used on American Dodge trucks. The example shown here is a tipper and Chrysler petrol or Perkins diesel engines were normally fitted.

The Dodge Commando 2 was introduced in 1981 with a range of eight rigid models from 7.3ton, as illustrated, to 16ton. There were also three tractor units from 18 to 26ton. The series 2 have a larger radiator grille.

Above:
An earlier model of the Commando 100 (series 1), which shows the smaller radiator grille. This is a 26ton tractor unit. *VRPL*

Centre left:
A 1983 Commando 100 (series 2) four-wheel rigid 16ton vehicle which is fitted with a Perkins T6 3544 six-cylinder diesel engine.

Bottom left:
The Dodge 300 series is an import from Spain (the 275hp 38ton Barreiros) and was available until 1982 as a rigid or tractor unit. *VRPL*

ERF 1932-To date

Edwin R. Foden broke away from the family Foden concern and started to make his own diesel-powered lorries in 1933 using some proprietary units such as Jennings cabs and Gardner engines. The first vehicle was forward-control four-wheeler for a 6ton payload (type C14) and the model proved so successful that it remained in production until 1946. All ERF vehicles since that time have been forward-control and have had conventional radiator grilles and the prewar range catered for 6ton to 15ton payloads on rigid four-, six-or eight-wheeled chassis.

The range continued after the war but with a redesigned radiator grille which was larger and almost flush with the slightly curved cab front which had lower windscreens. Then followed a more streamlined cab with wrap-round windscreen which was introduced in 1949.

In 1952 a completely new design of oval radiator grille was incorporated on all models and this lasted until about 1961 when the LV cab type was introduced. The company produced its first 32ton gcw tractor unit in 1962.

The production of fire appliances was commenced in 1967 and this lasted for 10 years until it was taken over by Jennings, which had always had close links with ERF, as Cheshire Fire Engineering Ltd.

In 1970 the A range was rationalised and in 1974 the B range with steel-framed plastic cabs appeared for the highly successful four-, six-, and eight-wheeled rigids and for the four- and six-wheeled tractor units for load of up to 32ton gtw which appeared in 1975. With the increasing use of

British lorries on the continent, ERF developed the SP cab in 1973 on vehicles up to 42ton gcw with the Motor Panels sleeper cab as an optional extra.

A lighter version of the B range known as the M range was introduced in 1978 which had the same cab but was a four-wheel 16ton gtw with the option of a Gardner or Dorman engine; this was followed by a six-wheel 26ton rigid. Production of the B range continued until it was superseded by the C range introduced in 1981. The C range was in production for only five years when the models were upgraded with the E range in 1986.

In 1983 ERF introduced a new lightweight 16tonner, the M16 model, powered by a Perkins diesel as standard, and this four-wheeler was available with five different wheelbases. The model was discontinued in 1986.

For some reason, there was no D range, whether to avoid confusion with the then popular Ford D range is not known, but the E series was introduced in 1986 and has proved most successful. All are fitted with the Cummins turbo-charged diesel engine, although a Gardner can be fitted in the lower weight carrying models. The option of a six- or nine-speed synchromesh gearbox is available, and a new design of cab is fitted to some of the four-wheelers. The multi-wheelers and the tractor units can have four different cab options, namely:

Below:
The classic prewar design of ERF is still very much apparent on this 15ton payload twin-steering lorry delivered in 1953.

Above:
The cab design favoured in 1954 is shown on this 15ton eight-wheeled platform lorry. The oval radiator grille is distinctive to ERF at that time. The 18ft wheelbase accommodates a 24ft long body.

short day, day, night or full sleeper. There are different wheelbases for the E range of models which cover 16ton gvw to 32ton gvw for the rigids and 38ton for the tractor units.

Since the B series in 1974, ERF have adopted the SP cab which is constructed with a steel inner framework on which a sheet moulded compound (SMC) plastic replaceable panels are attached. This enables ERF to give an eight year anti-corrosion guarantee in addition to providing a lightweight and clean cab. The latest cab is coded SP4A.

ERF is now the only British owned commercial vehicle manufacturers, apart from Dennis (which is concentrating on passenger and municipal vehicles) and one or two small concerns.

The past 10 years has seen the company continue to modernise its range and keep pace with the competition from continental manufacturers and technical improvements. The recession has, of course, had an impact on ERF, as it has on every other industry, and plans for a second factory had to be abandoned. Fortunately, tentative plans of a working agreement with the Japanese Hino organisation in 1983 were dropped and ERF has continued to be independent.

Below:
An ERF tractor with a Dyson low-loading semi-trailer for heavy haulage.

Above:

A type LAC 340 tractor powered by a Cummins oil engine delivered in 1974 for a well-known haulier of liquids. This was the first vehicle to be painted in the operator's new livery of red and green with yellow lettering.

Below:

The new B series appeared in 1975. This rigid eight-wheeled tipper is powered by a Gardner 6LXB diesel engine through a David Brown six-speed gearbox and double reduction rear axle. The body is 23ft 6in long and the sides are 4ft 6in high.

Below:

A Gardner-powered ERF tractor is the motive unit for this special tanker for the transport of corrosive liquids. The tanks are of nickel steel equipped with a heating blanket covering the entire tank barrel to keep the contents fluid in low-temperature conditions.

Bottom:

A 1981 tractor unit fitted with a Gardner 6LXCT turbocharged engine developing 230bhp at 1,900rpm.

Above:

This ERF C series (C36) tractor unit has a wheelbase of 9ft 10in and is coupled to a semi-trailer used to demonstrate to dealers the uses of Spicer transmission.

Below:

A C series (C40) 6x2 tractor unit and semi-trailer seen discharging animal feed into silos at Buxted's chicken farm complex near Thetford, Norfolk, in 1984.

Top:
In 1985 Mr Kipling (the cake division of Rank Hovis MacDougall) took delivery of seven ERF C series 4x2 tractor units plated at 28tonne. They are fitted with Gardner 6LXCT turbocharged diesel engines developing 223bhp at 1,900rpm. This power is transmitted through a Fuller 13-speed gearbox to a Rockwell 3.7:1 rear drive axle.

Above:
The E series was introduced in 1986. This E10 tractor unit of 1987 and semi-trailer is engaged in quarry work.

Right:
This C57 tractor has been uprated to 100tonne. It is powered by a Cummins NTE350 turbocharged diesel developing 332bhp at 1,900rpm. It is equipped with a nine-speed Eaton Fuller gearbox, Kirkstall rear bogie and a standard ERF SMC day cab. It is seen here passing through Telford carrying a 55ton crane, the load being 19ft high and 17ft 2in wide. *VRPL*

Above:
The M series lightweight rigids were introduced in 1983. This shows the 25G3 six-wheel chassis with ZF six-speed synchromesh overdrive gearbox. The ERF non-reactive bogie ensures that the forward rear axle does not lift on braking with consequent loss of grip. *VRPL*

Left:

New in 1987 this E12 tractor unit is equipped with a Gardner turbocharged diesel engine.

Below:

Six ERF M16 series 16tonne rigids joined the British Aerospace fleet in 1985. The M16 series has a lightweight SMC tilt cab, and the low chassis height of 37½in makes for easy loading and unloading. These two vehicles are fitted with Perkins T6 354.4 turbocharged diesel engines developing 140bhp. *VRPL*

Foden 1899-To date

Edwin Foden designed his first steam tractor in 1882 using an efficient design of compound engine and it came into regular production from about 1887. Within 10 years load-carrying steam lorries were on the market and in 1902 production of the famous 5ton lorry commenced which ran until 1923, The superiority of the petrol (and later oil) engine, plus the heavy legislation placed on steam vehicles sounded their death knell and so in 1931 the company turned its attentions to diesel-powered lorries using the Gardner engine, but later using several different makes of oil engine.

In the eight years up to the outbreak of World War 2 a large number of commercial vehicles were produced ranging from 4ton to 15ton payload and all featuring the same distinctive but conventional design of radiator grille. During the war the company was engaged on supplying 6x4 army lorries and parts for Centaur and Crusader tanks as well as munitions of various types.

Civilian production commenced as soon as possible after the cessation of hostilities using the prewar types but the cab design was soon modernised with a curved front with the radiator grille blending into the new outline.

In 1964 the Steel Company of Wales placed an order for a large-capacity tip lorry, as a result of which the first of many giant dump trucks were manufactured. The particular model looks small by comparison with those manufactured in later years,

but at the time was regarded as huge. In the same year the revolutionary Foden two-stroke diesel engine was produced and production continued until 1977. Further modernisation and development took place in 1956 when power-assisted steering was introduced and two years later Foden unveiled its first vehicles fitted with a reinforced plastic cab, which in 1960 was modified to tilt forward and give complete and unobstructed access to the engine and mechanical components. In 1968 a few

Below:
Delivered c1953 this twin-steer 15ton lorry has the standard prewar Foden cab.

half cabs with forward angled windscreens mounted low on the chassis were made for special orders for cranes and the carriage of long girders etc.

A new factory was opened in 1974 for increased production, although later the company ran into financial difficulties, but a large NATO order effected a recovery. New Fleetmaster and Haulmaster models with steel tilt cabs (of Motor Panels manufacture) were introduced in 1977. The Fleetmaster was normally fitted with a Cummins or Rolls-Royce 290bhp engine and the Haulmaster which had a slightly different radiator grille and a split windscreen, was fitted with Cummins, Gardner or Rolls-Royce 18-265bhp engine. These models were also available in 1979 with a glass-fibre and aluminium cab.

In 1980 following a year of financial difficulties the receivers were called in and after negotiations the American company Paccar International (builders of Kenworth and Pacific trucks in the USA) acquired control. The new company is now called Sandbach Engineering Co although the familiar Foden name still appears on all the vehicles.

Just before the take-over Foden had launched the S10 series, and these models were continued and improved over the years, and the present range of 3000 and 4000 models is basically similar in appearance.

The 3000 range includes six- and eight-wheel rigids and 4x2 tractor units with a choice of wheelbases and an option of 8, 10 and 12litre engines of either Perkins or Cummins manufacture. This range is for up to 32tonnes.

The 4000 range includes both three and four axle rigids and tractor units of varying options (4x2, 6x2, 4x2 with tag axle and 6x4) and is designed for 32tonnes and upwards. Cummins or Caterpillar engines are fitted as standard. Both the 3000 and 4000 range share the same cab design.

A new 2000 range has now been introduced for the 17.8tonne GVW market and this features a new glass fibre (GRP) composite cab. This four-wheeler is available in seven different lengths of wheelbase and is powered by either the Cummins 180bhp engine or the Perkins 210bhp engine. Eaton nine-speed or ZF six-speed gearboxes can be fitted and there is a choice of final drive rear axles.

The latest innovation from Foden is a new fully electronic air suspension system for their twin-steer tractors, while the cab interiors have also been completely redesigned.

Above:
The postwar redesigned cab and radiator grille shown on a FG5/15 model eight-wheeled platform lorry.

Below:
Keeping a similar style of radiator embellishment this 1958 short-wheelbase eight-wheeler has the rounded type cab.

Top:
From cement in bulk to cement in sacks! This 16/24 model was powered by a Gardner oil engine and had a five-speed overdrive gearbox. The tyres are 40 by 8.

Above:
An unusual Foden van fitted with a four-cylinder two-stroke diesel engine.

Top right:
Foden made several vehicles with half-cabs. This dump-truck is on demonstration work in a quarry typical of the conditions for which it was designed.

Centre right:
This Superhaulmaster six-wheeled tipper has a Cummins engine and the Foden S90 all-steel cab. A model of the 1980s.

Below:
The Foden S10 sleeper-cab is fitted to this tractor unit delivered in 1979 for long distance haulage. It is powered by a Rolls-Royce 265L diesel engine driving through a Fuller gearbox. The trailer length is 38ft 8in.

Below:
The Haulmaster models were introduced in 1978 as improved versions of earlier models and were fitted with an all-steel cab. This 1978 rigid 30ton eight-wheeler is fitted with a Gardner 6LXC diesel engine developing 210bhp and a Foden eight-speed gearbox. The model illustrated has Edbro ED16 tipping gear with a Wilcox all-aluminium welded 30cu yd body. *VRPL*

Left:
The new Foden cabs tilt to 75° and it is no longer necessary to lift the front grille or adjust the gearstick. *VRPL*

Above:
The clean lines of the new Foden S10 cab introduced in 1980. *VRPL*

Left:
This 1983 Foden 6x4 tractor unit is powered by a Rolls-Royce Eagle 290L six-cylinder 12litre diesel engine. *VRPL/Perkins*

Overleaf:
One of 10 in a fleet of 33 vehicles operated by Dougal Transport in 1984. It is powered by the Rolls-Royce Eagle 265Li six-cylinder diesel engine developing 265bhp. *VRPL/Perkins*

Above:
The Fleetmaster rigid eight assembly line in the works at Sandbach. *VRPL*

Below:
A 1982 Foden S106 rigid six for a cement mixer. The S10 cab is fitted and it has a Gardner 6LXCT engine with Fuller nine-speed gearbox and super low crawler gear. The front axle is by GKN and the rear bogie is by Rockwell. *VRPL*

Ford 1908-To date

Ford began to export its American cars to England in 1904 followed four years later by the model T lorry, but from 1911 assembly of these began at the company's premises at Trafford Park, Manchester. The model T continued until 1927 when the Ford model A was introduced. A move to Dagenham in Essex took place in 1931 and from then onwards the vehicles were of English design (more or less) and manufacture.

The Ford contribution to the war effort was immense, making Bren-gun carriers and other half-tracked vehicles, the general service 15cwt trucks and 4x4 forward-control three-tonners for the army and the other services. It also produced the six-wheel winch lorries for the balloon barrage, mobile canteens and fire tenders.

The name Fordson was adopted for commercial vehicles from about 1929 and another change of name occurred in late 1939 when the word Thames was introduced In 1957 this became Thames Trader, a name which continued for the next eight years.

The Thames 15cwt forward-control van made its appearance in the mid-1950s and this was the forerunner of the highly successful Transit van which was produced in 1965 and developed from German Ford Taunus vehicles. The original production was in Belgium with assembly at Langley near Slough. The vans were revamped in 1978 and are still in production. The bonneted Thames Trader K series was also introduced in the early 1960s with a range from 2ton to 8ton, some models being available with several different wheelbases. The K-series remained in production until 1972.

The D-series of forward-control vehicles made its appearance in 1965 catering for loads from 5 ton to 28 ton including a short-wheelbase tractor for use with semi-trailers. The range was redesigned in 1978 and continued in production until 1981 when the new Cargo range was announced. The Ford A series, which was never as successful, ceased production in 1983.

Ford's first venture into the really heavy duty market was the H series 'Transcontinental' range (32ton to 44ton) introduced in 1975, but this was not really a British vehicle for the engine came

Below:
A Ford Thames van of 2ton payload which could have either a petrol or diesel engine fitted. A 3ton van had similar dimensions but was fitted with larger tyres and servo-assisted brakes.

from Cummins, the gearbox from Fuller, axles from Rockwell, cab assembly from Berliet (later absorbed by Renault) and the whole collection assembled in Amsterdam. In 1982, when the Amsterdam plant closed, the final assembly was undertaken at Sandbach Engineering (Foden) while the cabs were painted at the old Karrier factory in Dunstable. The vehicles never enjoyed a great success as they faced considerable competition from other foreign manufacturers and the range was discontinued in 1983.

In July 1986 Iveco (Industrial Vehicles Corporation), the commercial vehicle wing of Fiat (into which had already been merged OM, Unic and Magirus Deutz) took control of all the Ford commercial vehicles over 3.5tonnes and from that time onwards the products were badged as Iveco.

The Ford Cargo models superseded the D series in 1981, and the range extended from 6ton to

Above:
The Ford Thames 15cwt van popular with the small retailer in the late 1950s and early 1960s was the forerunner of the Transit van.

Left:
Who said glamour and commercial vehicles don't mix! A Transit van shows its graceful lines! The Transit series is based on six different payload categories, the larger versions having twin rear wheels.

Left:
A 5ton Thames Trader tractor unit of 9ft wheelbase powered by a six-cylinder diesel engine. This semi-forward control cab was used on many models in the Thames Trader range for several years.

Right:
A Ford D-series box van of 1972 which weighs under 3ton unladen and thus does not need a driver with a heavy goods vehicle licence.

8ton, including 4x2 tractor units, all with a variety of wheelbase and predominantly fitted with Cummins, Perkins or Deutz engines. The series can easily be distinguished by their deep quarter lights at the side of the cabs. The Cargo range was merged with Iveco when the change-over was made.

Ford's greatest success has been with the Transit van right from the time the first model was produced in 1965. The Transit was completely redesigned in 1986 with a new aerodynamic front end. Models are produced for loads from 15cwt to

Above:
A 16ton D-series fitted with a Ford 6litre turbocharged diesel engine. The wheelbase is 17ft 2in. Supplied in 1972 for the delivery of both barrel and bottle beers.

3.5ton. Altogether the Transit is now available in three different wheelbases, five body styles, seven different payloads and four engine options.

Ford have also continued with light vans based on their car chassis and engines.

201

Top right:
The A-series provides 3½-5½ton gvw vehicles which thus fit into the Ford range between the lighter Transits and the heavier D-series. This 3ton van is powered by the Ford 2.4litre diesel engine.

Centre right:
The Transcontinental articulated unit powered by a Cummins turbocharged engine with a Fuller nine-speed gearbox. The Transcontinental range is available in 4x2 and 6x4 variants with a choice of wheelbases.

Below:
The latest Ford is the Cargo with a range from 6ton to 28½ton gross with a choice of engines and transmissions. The deflector plate on the cab roof is to improve air-flow and is claimed to make a saving on fuel consumption. Such plates are now fitted to a great number of vehicles of all makes.

Above:
The Ford Transcontinental H range was discontinued in 1983 and this 1979 vehicles is a typical example of the series. Note that it is left-hand drive, although the vehicles were imported from the Netherlands in any case.
VRPL

Below:
The replacement for the Transcontinental H was the Cargo range. This 3220 32.5tonne unit is powered by a Deutz engine developing 220bhp. *VRPL*

Above left:
Another cargo tractor unit, this example is for 28ton and is powered by a Perkins V8 640 diesel engine. Atlas Express ordered 26 of these vehicles in 1983 for their trunk routes between depots. *VRPL*

Left:
A typical cargo van of 1983 in the 6ton class used by a well-known truck rental organisation. *VRPL*

Above:
R. Hind Ltd of Carlisle built the special bodywork on this 7½ton Cargo chassis in 1985. This shows the longest wheelbase available in the range — 4.975m (16ft 4in). The body is 7.2m (approximately 23ft 4in) long, and it can hold 2,500 books and audio cassettes. *VRPL*

Left:
One of 12 Cargo 2420 models supplied to Premix (a division of Amalgamated Roadstone Co). These 24ton 6x4s are powered by a Deutz F67L 413 V6 diesel which develop 206bhp and are fitted with an Eaton Fuller nine-speed gearbox. Standard equipment on all Tandem Cargo vehicles includes tachometer, tinted glass, exhaust brake, heated mirrors and driver's suspension seat. *VRPL*

Above:
This is the first Cargo 1624 model drawbar outfit to be fitted with the Cummins LT10 240bhp six-cylinder turbocharged diesel engine. The wheelbase is 16ft 3in and the body length is approx 20ft 9in. The maximum payload is 22tonnes. *VRPL*

Right:
An Iveco Cargo 2424 tipper, with a capacity of 24ton and fitted with a 240bhp engine. *VRPL*

Above:
The heaviest and largest in the range: a 3828 model for a gross weight of 38ton and fitted with a 280bhp engine. Although badged as a Ford, it is basically an Iveco. *VRPL*

Right:
The cab of the Iveco Turbo Star tractor unit. *VRPL*

Freight Rover 1981-To date

Following the 1968 merger of Leyland Motors with the British Motor Holdings (basically Austin and Morris), there was much badge swapping and interchange of designs and some were marketed as BMC. Later, as the Rover company had already entered the Leyland empire, the name changed to Freight Rover.

In 1981 the Freight Rover Sherpa van was introduced and this was basically the Leyland light van of 1975 available for payloads of 13, 18 and 22cwt with six body styles and the option of two different engines. The van was restyled in 1982 and then became more successful with 11 different models available, although still under severe competition from the Bedford CF and Ford Transit. By 1988 there were two body widths available and at the 1988 Motor Show the Sherpa was again improved with air suspension, and the 200 series was introduced (12 models being displayed) for loads from 13cwt up to 3.5tonne GVW.

As Freight Rover was a Leyland company, with the dismemberment of the former empire it passed under the control of DAF in 1987 and the Leyland-DAF badge is now seen on the later vehicles.

Above:
The Freight Rover Sherpa 200 model of 1987 was designed for a payload of 2,500kg (approximately 50cwt). It is fitted with a Perkins 211 series high-speed diesel engine, which is claimed will return 40mpg at a steady 60mph in top gear. *VRPL*

Left:
The Perkins two litre high-speed diesel as fitted in the Freight Rover Sherpa vans. The engine was developed jointly by Perkins and Freight Rover. *VRPL*

Guy 1918-1979

In 1914 Sydney Slater Guy left the Sunbeam Motor Co, where he was works manager, and started his own company, almost next door, to produce his own design of commercial vehicles. The new factory was engaged in wartime production almost immediately, but in 1920 vehicle manufacture commenced in earnest with the 25cwt J-type lorries, and later the four-wheel and six-wheel models for 7-12ton payloads. In the early 1930s the Wolf range for 25cwt to 3ton was produced and the 3/4ton Vixen and the 6ton Otter models made their appearance.

The government ordered large numbers of the angular fronted Quad-ant 4x4 tractors for war use and also allowed Guy to produce a few vehicles for the civilian market to those operators who could claim an urgent need and who had priority.

Full civilian production recommenced after 1947 to prewar designs, but in 1952 a new all-steel cab was fitted to the 6ton Otter model and the following year this vehicle was available as a short wheelbase tractor for use with semi-trailers. A year later the Big Otter was produced for 8ton loads together with the Invincible range of four-, six- and eight-wheeled rigid vehicles for 12ton, 20ton and 24ton gcw respectively.

In 1956 the Warrior range was introduced; these were forward-control types for 6ton to 15ton payloads as either rigid or articulated units. From 1958 they shared the same design of cab as the Invincible.

Guy Motors was taken over by Jaguar Cars in 1961, which in turn was taken over by Leyland Motors in 1968. In the interim the Big J series of six and eight-wheeled rigids and tractive units appeared, being a development of some previous models.

Alas, production finally ceased in 1979, and the famous Red Indian figure with the slogan 'Feathers in our Cap' no longer adorns the radiators of products from Fallings Park, Wolverhampton and such radiator caps are now a treasured memento of the past.

Below:
This Guy Vixen 4ton platform lorry could carry 80 milk churns. It was supplied to its owners in 1951 and was practically identical to the prewar design.

The 1957 7ton Otter had the new style cab which was virtually the same as that fitted to some Thornycroft models.

An 8ton Warrior van fitted with a Meadows diesel engine and delivered in 1956.

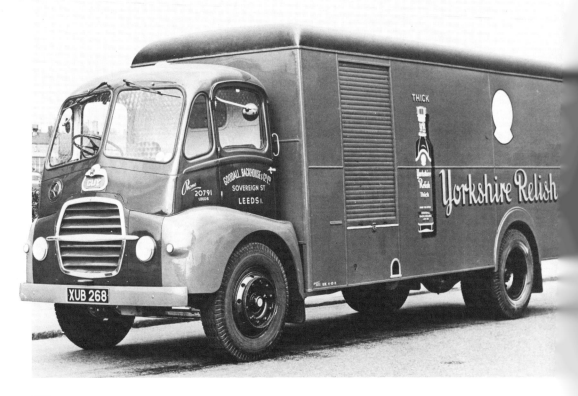

Top:
A Warrior articulated unit, fitted with the AEC 7.7litre diesel engine.

Above:
A different design of Warrior cab on this tractor unit which hauls a York Freightmaster semi-trailer.

A Big J tractor unit operating at 32ton gtw coupled to a tri-axle semi-trailer milk tanker.

Another Big J tractor unit fitted with a Cummins engine and operating at 30ton gtw. The wide loading side door of the semi-trailer permits pallet loading as shown.

International 1965-1969

In 1965 the Doncaster factory of International Harvester which produced farm machinery commenced vehicle production of Loadstar trucks of a normal-control design. This was based on the American International Paystar, but was modified to comply with UK Construction and Use regulations although fitted with many parts imported from the USA. A few 4x2 rigids were built, together with some articulated tractor units, and a forward-control model was also planned. However the vehicle project did not make sufficient profit and faced severe competition from the European imports; thus all production ceased in 1968.

Right:
An International K8 lorry of 6ton capacity in 1943. This vehicle was probably delivered to the UK as ckd (completely knocked down) and assembled here by the International organisation.

Above:
Front view showing the American influence of the International model manufactured in the UK in 1965.

Jensen 1938-1958

In the late 1930s the law stated that all vehicles weighing over 3ton unladen must be restricted to a maximum speed of 20mph. Therefore in 1938/39 Jensen Motors of West Bromwich, in collaboration with the Reynolds Tube Company, introduced some lightweight vehicles. These made use of light alloys and aluminium, Ford petrol engines and some parts from the then current Ford 3ton models to produce a lorry which was below 3ton unladen yet could carry a 6ton load at over 20mph.

In 1946 a fresh approach was made. The integral construction of the main frame and the superstructure as one unit in special light alloys allowed the vehicle to have a platform length of 23ft, which could accommodate a 1,632cu ft pantechnicon body on the 16ft 2in wheelbase in an overall length of 27ft 6in — the maximum permitted. Perkins P6 six-cylinder 70bhp oil engines were fitted behind the decorative radiator grille. It also had the advantage that the entire engine complete with radiator, clutch and gearbox could be withdrawn in 30min and a new unit fitted within a two-hour period.

The raising of speed limits and other legislation made the lightweight vehicles unnecessary, and this, plus the high cost of repairs if a vehicle was involved in an accident, proved to be their downfall.

In 1951 Jensen introduced a four-wheel articulated tractor and trailer called the Jen-Tug. This used the Austin A40 private car engine but the vehicles were not popular and few were built.

Production of Jensen Commercial Vehicles ceased in 1956/57 although the company continued to produce some high-class motorcars.

Below:
A typical Jensen 6ton payload lorry with light alloy bodywork. The length of the dropside body was 23ft.

Above:
**This large removal van was fitted with a
Perkins P6 diesel engine and was delivered in
1947. The number plate was obviously for
photographic purposes!**

Karrier 1908-1980

Karrier has had a chequered career since it began life in 1908 when Clayton & Company (Engineers) of Huddersfield introduced its first lorry under that name. Karrier Motors, as a separate entity, was founded in 1920 to continue the motor business and produced a wide range of types including in 1930 the Karrier Cob three-wheel tractor (a mechanical horse) and the Road-Railer bus for the London Midland & Scottish Railway in 1932. However financial difficulties in 1934 caused the company to be taken over by the Rootes Group a year later. Production of commercial vehicles was transferred to Luton and Dunstable alongside the Commer range. A popular prewar model was the Bantam which was designed for payloads up to 2ton and had a low loading height.

During the war a large number of 3ton 4x4 lorries (the K6 type), the KT4 4x4 gun tractor and some rigid six-wheel 3 tonners were built.

The peacetime vehicles were again produced after the war, the Bantam 30cwt and 2ton models having a new cab, while the CK3 model in the 3-4ton range was introduced, but in 1950 these were superseded by the Gamecock with underfloor engine and an all-steel cab identical to that fitted to some Commer vehicles.

In 1963 the Bantam was again updated. The whole of the Karrier range was popular for municipal duties and for suburban collection and delivery services.

The control of Karrier (likewise Commer) passed to Chrysler UK Ltd in 1973 and the firm is now owned by Renault/Peugeot which took over the Chrysler European operations, and is now merged with Dodge.

Below:
A 1946 Karrier CK3 model ¾ton dropside lorry with 14ft 6in by 6ft 8in body on 11ft wheelbase chassis. This is the same as the prewar design and continued for another three years.

Above:
An actual exhibit at the Commercial Motor Show in 1952 was this Bantam 2ton mineral water lorry. The cab has been modernised from the earlier models by incorporating rear corner lights and swivelling quarter lights in the all steel cab.

Left:
Another example of a Bantam two-tonner, this time with bodywork for a mobile shop, a role for which it was particularly suited.

Top:
A Bantam used as a tractive unit and fitted with the Commer diesel engine. It was used for delivery to a retail grocery chain.

Above:
One of the later production models of the Bantam, supplied to British Railways for parcels delivery.

Land Rover 1949-To date

The Rover Company produced its first car in 1904 but had never entered the commercial vehicle field. During World War 2 it manufactured many vehicles for the War Department. Afterwards, in 1949, the British Army sought a vehicle similar to the American Jeep, which had proved so successful in numerous wartime campaigns and served in many countries with the British and Allied Forces.

In 1949, therefore the first Land Rover four-wheel-drive vehicle, with a 7ft 4in wheelbase (11ft 11in long), made its appearance. It was powered by a 1,600cc petrol engine and had a payload of 15cwt. In 1952 a longer wheelbase (9ft 1in) version was introduced and a 2litre engine could be offered as an alternative. In 1957 a 2.1litre Rover diesel engine was also made available, and shortly afterwards the 2litre units were increased in size to 2¼litre. Land Rovers have been supplied for various bodies, including trucks, hard-tops, caravans, estate vehicles, fire appliances etc. A forward-control version is also available.

In 1970 the Range-Rover was introduced again with four-wheel drive — permanently engaged — and powered by a 130hp V8 petrol engine. This is extensively used by police forces in the UK for accident and traffic control work, where its high speed proves an advantage.

The Rover Company became part of the British Leyland empire in 1967.

Below:
A normal Land Rover fitted with a metal body — the canvas tilt body was standard — and available with either a petrol or diesel engine.

Above:
The long-wheelbase version of the Land Rover shown here with a station wagon body. It is fitted with the Rover V8 petrol engine.

Below:
The forward-control model Land Rover which gave increased load capacity and could still traverse rough terrain.

Left:
The forward-control chassis fitted with security van bodywork. Note the comparatively short wheelbase for this type of vehicle.

Above:
The Range Rover station wagon is used by many police forces especially for motorway patrols and for accidents etc. They can carry a large amount of useful equipment.

Leyland 1907-To date

The vast British Leyland Truck and Bus Division, which has swallowed up so many manufacturers, began making steam wagons in 1896, the first petrol-engined vehicle appearing in 1904 for a 30cwt payload. Then followed the Y-type 3ton and the X-type 3½ton in 1907. The firm established itself in 1912 with the normal-control 3ton subsidy-type vehicle, of which 5,932 were built up to November 1918 for the Royal Flying Corps, the vehicle became known as the RAF type and was sold to many civilian operators.

Leyland has been responsible for many developments in the commercial field over the years, backed by a team of brilliant engineers such as Sir Harry Spurrier, and it thus gained a great reputation for good design and reliability. In the 1930s Leyland was producing freight vehicles with a range extending from the Cub 3ton normal-control model to the eight-wheeled forward-control Octopus for 15ton payloads. Other models were named Bison, Buffalo, Bull, Beaver, Hippo, Lynx and Steer.

During the war years Leyland contributed to the national effort by producing five different types of tank including the Cromwell and Comet as well as supplying 1,000 Hippos and other vehicles and munitions for the fighting services.

One of the first of the new postwar range was the Comet 75 in 1947 — a semi-forward-control 6ton model distinguished by the new frontal styling. Four years later the Comet 90 model for 7½ton loads was made and remained in production until 1960. Super Comet forward-control models appeared in 1954, with cab design similar to that of the Albion Chieftain.

In 1951 Leyland acquired Albion Motors, followed by Scammell in 1955 and AEC (which had already acquired Maudslay, Crossley and Thornycroft) in 1962. Leyland acquired a major shareholding in Bristol Commercial Vehicles in 1965, Rover/Alvis joined the empire in 1966, followed by Aveling-Barford a year later and in 1968 Leyland merged with British Motor Holdings which already had Austin, Morris, Guy and Daimler under its wing. Thus many famous makers have disappeared under the Leyland name.

A completely new design of cab was introduced in 1968 known as Ergomatic and this became standard on the heavier models in the range, including those produced under the Albion and AEC names.

In 1970 the goods vehicle range was again extended with the introduction of the Bear six-wheeler and two years later the new Buffalo range of models up to 32ton. The Marathon range of tractive units and 4x2 rigids for loads up to 32ton gcw or 44ton gtw were introduced in 1973 and

Below:

A Leyland Octopus of 1950 vintage with a special body for the carriage of flour in bulk. The payload of 8ton of flour could be discharged in 45min by compressed air.

three years later there was a new Octopus rigid eight-wheeler.

The lighter vehicles known since 1968 as the Redline range were redesigned in 1972 with the Mastiff six-wheeler joining the existing Mastiff (16, 24 and 28ton), the Boxer (10-16ton) and the Terrier (6½-9½ton). These vehicles were all fitted with the G cab design. The range also incorporated the GF range of lighter vehicles from BMC of 3½-6½ton. All these models were produced at the Bathgate Works, West Lothian.

One of the latest 1980 designs from Leyland is the Roadtrain (model T45) with five models of forward-control tractive units incorporating a new cab design (type C40) which can also be supplied as a sleeper cab, and the new Leyland Flexitorque engine with Rolls-Royce or Cummins as an alternative.

At the same time there is a normal-control Landtrain of which eight models are available from 19ton to 65ton. The models are mainly for the export market and supersede the Super Hippo and Super Beaver.

In 1981 a lighter version of the Roadtrain, called the Cruiser, entered production with a range of

three tractive units fitted with a slim version of the new C40 cab and designed for operation up to 34ton gcw. Later that year a lightweight range, also fitted with the C40 cab, called the Freighter was introduced to replace the Clydesdale, and from late-1982 the Boxer.

From 1982 Leyland started to discontinue the Redline range, beginning with the Terrier 4-6ton in May, followed by the Mastiff 11ton model in September 1983 and finally the Boxer 6-11ton in March 1984.

The Blueline range — the Buffalo, Bison and Lynx — had all ceased production by 1982, as had the Clydesdale range. The last of the old Leyland/Albion range to disappear was the Chieftain, which had been introduced in 1978 and was withdrawn in December 1983.

The replacement was the T45 Freighter range introduced in November 1981 for 16ton gvw and available in five different wheelbase models along with a choice of four engines. A year later models for 12.3ton gvw and 13.29ton gvw, followed in August 1983 by models in the 10.81 and 14.75ton gvw ranges. Again all models were available with differing wheelbases and a choice of engines.

The lighter models were replaced by the T45 Roadrunner range from 6-10ton in 1984. The range offered four/five different wheelbase lengths from 10ft 8in to 14ft. All models had a BMC 6.98 engine, but this was later changed to a Leyland engine when the old Bathgate plant closed in 1986. All models have the Motor Panels cab.

The ex-Scammell Constructor S26 6x4 24ton and 8x4 30ton chassis, now fitted with Cummins 11litre engines, continued to be available. The model was first introduced in 1980 but it has been supplied with many different engines, the last being the Perkins Eagle Turbo-charged diesel rated at 285bhp.

At the Motor Show in 1986 Leyland exhibited a fire appliance — the first for 25 years. Based on the 16ton Freighter chassis with a Leyland 400 series engine and automatic transmission. It is believed that only a few were ever built. The 4x2 Cruiser lightweight tractor unit for 32ton gvw was also on view.

Above left:
The Super Comet forward control was introduced in 1954. This van has illuminated panels made from acrylic sheet.

Below left:
At the lighter end of the Leyland range is the Terrier with a choice of engines.

Above:
With the same G-type cab design as the Terrier, this Boxer is a 1980 model with a turbocharged engine. The vehicle covers over 1,000 miles a week and the wind deflector on the cab roof is intended to make some considerable fuel economy returns, especially on long motorway runs.

Above:
A 1980 Bison 24ton six-wheeled tipper. The alloy body for sand and rock haulage carries a payload of 16½ton and a capacity of 12cu m.

News of talks to merge Leyland with General Motors circulated towards the close of 1986, for Leyland were making redundancies in its workforce and did not have the finances to design and produce a replacement for its Roadtrain range, a range which had been built since 1980. However, it came as a shock when, in February 1987, it was announced that DAF had taken control of Leyland. The DAF influence made itself felt very soon afterwards, with the closure of the old Scammell plant at Watford. Some of the factories at Leyland were also closed. In addition, DAF components started to be used and vehicles started to appear with a 'Leyland-DAF' badge.

Above:
Introduced in 1980 this new Leyland Constructor (part of the T45 Roadtrain range) which will supersede the Routeman and Octopus models. This 30ton gross eight-wheeler carries a 20ton payload in the Metalair bulk cement tank fitted with a Holmes blower. The engine develops 209bhp and is matched to the Easton six-speed gearbox.

Below:
P&O Road Services Ltd took delivery of 11 Marathon tractor units in April 1978. Fitted with Cummins diesel engines they haul semi-trailers carrying chemicals.

SUPERIOR INTERNATIONAL L1

Top:
One of the 1980 Leyland models is the Landtrain, developed chiefly for the export market. Several variations are available.

Above:
An extremely long semi-trailer is hauled by this 1980 Leyland Roadtrain tractive unit. The vehicle has the C40 cab, a Leyland TL12 turbocharged engine developing 281bhp and a Spicer 10-speed gearbox.

**This Roadtrain hauls a
semi-trailer which holds
40cu yd — payload
capacity of 20½ton — of
bulk grain.**

**The 1981 introduction was the Cruiser fitted
with a 'slim' version of the C40 cab for
operation up to 34ton gcw. Three tractive units
are available.**

Above:
The EA type van was introduced in BMC days for payloads of 3½-4½ton.

Below:
The Sherpa van has been universally popular since it was introduced in 1976. The model illustrated has left hand drive and is operated by a Netherlands butcher. It has a payload of one ton and can be fitted with either petrol, lpg or diesel engine of 1,798cc capacity. The Sherpa received a facelift in 1982.

Left:
**Drawbar trailers, a
common sight on the
roads of the 1930s and
1940s, are again coming
into fashion. This Leyland
Mastiff MS1600, for an
11ton payload, of 1979
complete with air
deflector, makes
considerable savings in
distribution costs.** *VRPL*

Above:
These two Leyland Boxer BX1600 (11ton payload, 16ton gvw) are fitted with the Leyland 6.98 turbocharged engine developing 137bhp and have Dobson bodies on extended chassis.

Right:
Badged as Leyland, the old Scammell Constructor was still constructed in the early to mid-1980s. This example is fitted with the Leyland TL11A 209bhp turbocharged engine. The Hydro hoist steel body holds 30cu yd. *VRPL*

Above:
The 11ton payload, 16ton gvw Clydesdale models were available in five different wheelbases and could be fitted with four different Leyland engines.

Below:
A typical example of a 1980 Terrier van for eight ton payloads. This range was produced from 1970 to 1984.

**Like the Clydesdale, the
Reiver was another old
Albion name, but the
similarity ends there! The
six-wheeler has a 22-
24ton gvw and Leyland
144bhp turbocharged
engines were initially
fitted but these were
updated with the 150bhp
turbocharged engine in
1979.**

Top right:

The Leyland Roadtrain is part of the T45 range and was introduced in 1980 for a 32-37.4 gcw. Two wheelbase versions were offered 9ft 8½in or 10ft 6¾in. Leyland, Cummins, Rolls-Royce or Perkins engines were available.

Centre right:

Another part of the Leyland T45 range is the Roadrunner introduced in 1984 with three capacities — 3.39ton gvw, 7.37ton gvw and 9.84ton gvw. Four wheelbase lengths are available and a choice of four Leyland engines. This is a 7.5tonne — new weight ratings came in 1987 — van fitted with a Leyland 130bhp naturally aspirated engine, on a 3.2m wheelbase. Ventilated disc brakes of 315mm diameter are fitted to the front axle. *VRPL*

Below:

Since DAF took control of Leyland the Roadrunner has been redesigned. This is the 7.5tonne version in its new form, which is marketed as Leyland-DAF. *VRPL*

Above:
The Leyland-DAF series 95, 38ton gcw unit of 1988. *VRPL*

Below:
One of the very few Leyland Freighter (16ton chassis) fire appliances supplied to Lancashire County Fire Brigade in 1986.

Maudslay 1903-1954

The name Maudslay is well-known among engineering circles of yesteryear for the family became established in marine and steam engines as far back as 1835. It is associated with the beginnings of the Standard cars, and commercial vehicles bearing the Maudslay name were first produced in 1907, being chain-driven for 1½ton and 3ton capacity.

However the company was hit by the depression of the early 1930s and production dropped to a mere 50 vehicles a year. New designs were to have been shown at the cancelled Commercial Motor Show of 1939, but after the war these models were put into production. The range consisted of the Mogul, a 6ton four-wheeler; the Militant, a 7cu yd tipper; the Mustang, a 10ton rigid twin steer six-wheeler; the Maharajah, a 13ton rigid six-wheeler; the Maharanee, a 13ton tractor unit and the Meritor (originally named the Mikado), a 15ton rigid eight-wheeler.

In 1948 Maudslay was absorbed into the Associated Commercial Vehicle group and for a few years afterwards produced vehicles to its new owner's specification, and although a few kept the Maudslay name, most had the AEC badge.

Production finally ceased in 1954.

Above:
A Maudslay Mogul Mk II of 1948 which follows the style of the other models in the range at that time.

Above:
A Mustang twin-steer six-wheeler with platform body. Note the black radiator shell.

Below:
A Maudslay Marathon coach chassis was used as the basis of the Harrington-bodied horsebox supplied to British Railways in 1949. It was the prototype for a well-known Dinky Toy model.

Morris Commercial 1924-1954

The name of William Morris, later Lord Nuffield, and the Bullnose Morris are legendary and although the first light vans were produced on private car chassis from 1913, it was not until 1924 that the first real commercial vehicles bearing the name Morris came into being. The first model was a 1ton normal-control type with a 13.95hp four-cylinder petrol engine on a 10ft 2in wheelbase chassis which remained in production until 1932; by a strange coincidence it was designated as the model T — the same as the Ford. Other types quickly followed and in the mid-1930s the models ranged from 10cwt to 5ton. Both normal- and forward-control types were available, some of which had a 'classic' appearance with a slightly pointed radiator grille.

From 1948 the range coped with heavier payloads still, whilst retaining its good looks. Several alternative engines were offered including the 100hp six-cylinder and a new diesel manufactured in association with Saurer.

The popular J-type forward-control van was first introduced in 1949 for 10cwt payloads and two years later the restyled 2/3ton and 5ton models were called Equiload.

In 1952 Morris merged with Austin to form the British Motor Corporation and standardisation began to take place although several Morris designs could be seen with the Austin badge. In 1953 the LD type 1ton and 1½ton vans were manufactured to a design that was finalised before the merger negotiations. See also the chapter on BMC.

Below:
This Morris Commercial LC4 series 1½ton drop-side truck is similar to the models made just prior to 1939. It was an improved version of the LC3 series.

Above:
**A Morris articulated unit delivered in 1957.
The whole unit weighed 10ton and could carry
2,400gal of ice-cream.**

Below:
**The FJ-series chassis and cab with Bonallack
light alloy Luton body. The body has a capacity
of 1,240cu ft closed by an alloy roller shutter
at the rear.**

Above:

Appearing in the mid-1960s Morris J4 10/12cwt vans were used by many traders. This one had an overall length of 13ft 3in, a width of 5ft 9½in and a height of 6ft 3⅞ with 7ft 2in wheelbase.

Centre right:

A strengthened 7ton chassis was the basis of this tipper/dumper delivered in 1959. It had a four-wheel drive conversion by Martin Harper of Guildford.

Bottom right:

The FG range was fitted with a cab which made reversing easy and made for safer exit on the 'traffic' side of the vehicle. This is a 1½ton truck which shows the angle of the doors. Other models were produced to 5ton payload.

Scammell 1919-1987

The name Scammell is automatically associated with articulated lorries, mechanical horses and heavy haulage. Scammell and Nephew started business as wheelwrights and coachbuilders before producing its first articulated lorry in 1919 utilising lessons and experience gained in World War 1. Scammell Lorries Ltd was founded in 1922 and began producing articulated tanker vehicles. In 1931 rigid six-wheelers were also added to the range and in the late 1920s the first of a long line of heavy and rugged tractor units appeared which were especially designed for the haulage of very heavy and out-of-gauge loads.

Scammell became famous in 1933 for the design and production of its mechanical horse, later the Scarab, which was updated in design in 1945 and continued in production until the 1960s, by which time it had acquired a glass-fibre cab.

During the war Scammell produced the Pioneer tractor which was used for tank transporters, recovery vehicles and artillery tractors, many of these being used by showmen when they were sold by the War Department after the hostilities. Scammell also produced a large number of heavy-duty trailer fire pumps.

In 1949/50 the ex-military Pioneer was redesigned for civilian use and named Mountaineer. Production of a well-designed range of rigid and tractor units was marketed during the next six years, but in 1955 Scammell was bought out by Leyland, which wisely kept the Watford plant in operation without radical or drastic changes.

The big 30ton bonneted Highwayman tractor introduced in the mid-1950s was updated in the late 1950s and re-rated as 24ton gcw. In 1960 the Handyman made its appearance, and this was modified in 1964 with an Italian-designed cab as fitted to others in the Scammell range at that time, such as the rigid eight-wheeled 24ton gvw Routeman which first appeared in 1960, the same year as the Trunker 6x4 tractor unit entered production, and this again was updated in 1964.

In 1970 the Crusader 4x2 tractor was introduced but does not appear to have been too successful.

Until the late 1980s Scammell remained the specialised division of Leyland producing heavy tractors and from the 1970s former Thornycroft models, such as the airport fire-fighting vehicle, the Nubian, and the Amazon 6x6 tractor for gross weights of up to 300ton and now fitted with the Leyland cab similar to the Landtrain series, were produced. Other current models included the Constructor and S26, covering a range from 24tonnes gvw to 300tonnes gcw, both of which featured the Leyland C40 cab. Unfortunately, the DAF take-over of Leyland in 1987 led to the closure of the Watford factory and the end of the Scammell name.

Below:
A classic Scammell tractor and semi-trailer supplied in 1954. It was later called the Highwayman. It had a Gardner six-cylinder engine and was popular with many operators. The tanker could carry 4,000gal of petroleum spirit and was under 22ton gross weight.

Top:
**Eight years on from the previous illustration
this Highwayman has the more modern cab
with wrap-round screen and increased
visibility at the lower corners. It was powered
by the Leyland O.680 diesel developing
181bhp. The 3,800gal tank was built by
Thompson Bros.**

Above:
**This Constructor model is hauling a 180ton
casting from Sheffield to Liverpool for
machining.**

Left:
The Contractor range was introduced in 1964 especially to meet the demands of the heavy haulage specialist. There were seven basic models either 6x4 or 6x6 and with a choice of engines and gearboxes.

Below:
A Routeman rigid-eight featuring the Michelotti-styled cab with was fitted to several models. This 30-tonner has an extended wheelbase, and handles loads of up to 17½ton. The Routeman can be fitted with several different engines and gearbox combinations.

Above:
A 1968 Trunker II operating with a tandem axle tipping trailer for a 32ton gcw. This version was powered by a Leyland engine but there were many variants.

Right:
A Crusader 6x4 tractor destined to be shown at the Commercial Motor Show in 1968. There was also a 4x4 version, and again there were many engine and gearbox options for the operator.

Above:

The familiar mechanical horse — the Scammell Scarab in its postwar form. These vehicles were always popular with the railway companies.

Below:

The Townsman was the replacement for the Scarab. This new unit had a glass fibre cab and a number of outstanding design and mechanical features.

Seddon 1938-1974

Entering the commercial vehicle manufacturing field in 1937, Foster and Seddon had previously been engaged in the distribution and repair of vehicles for some 18 years. Their first vehicle was a forward-control lightweight 6ton chassis fitted with a Perkins P6 diesel engine. It was just proving popular with operators when the war called a halt to further production. After the war the model reappeared and the firm became Seddon Lorries from 1947. The range was expanded and in 1950 a small 3ton lorry powered by a Perkins engine appeared and two years later a normal control 25cwt and 30cwt van (known as the 25 range) which incorporated many glass-fibre body panels was produced. This did not gain popularity, although the 3tonner remained in production until 1963.

Styling changes took place in 1956 when wrap-round windscreens were fitted and a year later some models could be obtained with plastic cab panels. The emphasis shifted to the heavier models and in 1956/7 a 14ton gvw chassis (the Mk 15) was put on the market. Heavier rigids entered production during 1965/5 with Motor Panels cabs while in 1967 a tractor unit for 28ton gross and 32ton appeared powered by Rolls-Royce or Gardner engines.

Seddon was able to take over the old-established firm of Atkinson in 1970 and within two years a new heavy range was designed. Vehicles were still using the Seddon name, but in 1974 the new concern was acquired by International Harvester and became Seddon Atkinson — see next chapter.

Below:
A Seddon 6ton platform lorry powered by a Perkins P6 diesel engine and following the basic design of the first Seddon produced.

Above:

A Mk 7 3ton tractor fitted with a Perkins P4 engine and coupled to a Carrimore low-loading semi-trailer used as a mobile showroom. The overall length of the unit was 33ft, it was 7ft 6in wide and the overall height was 10ft. It was supplied in 1954.

Below:

A Mk 7L 3ton four wheel platform lorry.

Above:
A DD8 model 8x4 with power assisted steering for a 16¼ton payload. It was fitted with the Gardner 6LX engine.

Below:
New in 1966 was the Seddon 16 tractor units. This version was powered by a Perkins V8 diesel engine producing 170bhp and with a wheelbase of 9ft 3in it operated at 25ton gvw.

Above:
The 13/4 model of 1965.5 had a 14ft 8in wheelbase, and was fitted with a body 21ft long by 8ft 6in high. It was designed for a payload in excess of 8ton.

Below:
The Seddon Mk 14 for 11ton gross weight. It was powered by a Gardner 4LK engine and was one of the last types of Seddon cab to be produced before the company amalgamated with Atkinson.

Seddon Atkinson 1974-To date

The American concern International Harvester already had a European interest in commercial vehicles as it acquired a stake in the Dutch concern DAF. It also made a small effort in the UK in 1965-69.

When it acquired Seddon Atkinson in 1974 the range was already well established and continued unaltered in spite of rumours that all models would have the same cab design as DAF. In 1975 new heavyweight four-, six- and eight-wheeled rigids in the 400 range were in production as well as a 4x2 articulated tractor unit for 32ton gcw. A year later a lighter four-wheel rigid for 17ton payload was offered being designated the 200 series and powered by the International D358 engine. The 300 series appeared in 1978 which was a six-wheeled rigid for 24ton gvw. In 1982 the 200, 300 and 400 series were superseded by the similar but improved 201, 301 and 401 respectively.

International Harvester also had shares in Enasa, a Spanish-owned vehicle manufacturer, and when, in the early 1980s, International Harvester suffered severe financial problems, a number of the overseas subsidiaries were sold off. Seddon Atkinson was sold to Enasa in 1984 and International Harvesters also sold its shareholding in the Spanish company.

The 201, 301 and 401 ranges from 1981/82 were continued into the mid-1980s with minor improvements and differing engine options. The cab interior was also modified and the gearbox linkage improved.

Below:
A Seddon Atkinson 200 series tipper for 16ton gvw with a 12ft 6in wheelbase. All the 200 series are equipped with an International D358 diesel engine developing 134bhp.

In 1986 the 201 was replaced by the 2-11, which is a rigid four-wheeler for 16-24ton payloads. The model is fitted with a Motor Panels cab and a Perkins Phaser engine with choice of turbocharging if required. The vehicle is available with four differing wheelbases. It is interesting to note that the 2-11 is the basis of the municipal vehicles, mainly refuse collectors, being manufactured by Britannia Trucks which are growing in popularity. The vehicle is designed for 20-22 payloads, in four- or six-wheel format and with two widths of cab (2.2m or 2.5m).

The 301 and 401 series were also redesignated 3-11 and 4-11 respectively in 1986.

Right:
In 1982 the 200 series of 16ton gvw vehicles was updated to become the 201 series. Four wheelbase variations are offered and a choice of six cylinder Perkins engines. This one as a 5,870cc, 148bhp turbocharged and intercooled engine. *VRPL*

Below:
The 300 series was produced from 1978 to 1987. This 24ton gvw six-wheel tipper has a carrimore insulated aluminium body. *VRPL*

Above:
An extremely long wheelbase (at least 18ft 6in) is seen on this Seddon Atkinson 200 series van. The fast access Kerbsider body is fitted with theft-resistant sides from light but stiff interfolding thermoplastic panels which jack-knife outwards when open but form a rigid wall when closed. *VRPL*

Right:
One of the new 2-11 series of Seddon Atkinson 16tonners. It is fitted with the Perkins Phaser 160 turbocharged engine of 6,000cc developing 153bhp. *Perkins/VRPL*

Above:
A series 200 16ton gvw van which has a 24ft long alloy body. It is one of seven supplied in May 1977.

Centre right:
The series 400 shown here has a 24ft long body and a 17ft 6in wheelbase to carry heavy test weights for the weighbridge industry. It is powered by a Gardner 6LXB engine, one of several options for the 400 series.

Bottom right:
A turbocharged Gardner engine developing 270bhp is fitted to this 1981 Series 400. All the 400 series have tilt cabs.

Sentinel 1906-1957

The Scottish engineering firm of Alley and McLellan established the Sentinel steam lorry in 1906 moving from Polmadie, Glasgow to Shrewsbury in 1918. The Sentinel quickly gained popularity and by the mid-1920s the company was producing a six-wheeler for a 15ton payload, while in the 1930s the vehicles had modern equipment such as electric speedometers, electric lights, power take-off and self-stoking boilers. Their speed and absence of noise was quite remarkable.

During the war the firm was prominent in experiments and the manufacture of gas-producer trailers to help overcome the diesel and petrol shortage.

The last steam wagons were produced in 1949 as an export order for the Argentine, the UK market having fallen since the late-1930s.

In the period covered by this book the firm concentrated on diesel lorries and from 1946 manufactured a four-wheel forward-control 7/8ton vehicle with underfloor engine. A few six-wheel chassis were also produced for a 10ton load. All the vehicles had the Sentinel-Ricardo horizontal diesel engine mounted on a frame behind the modern-looking cab.

In 1957 the firm was acquired by Transport Vehicles (Warrington) Ltd which took over the stocks of existing chassis, some of which were fitted with the Commer two-stroke engine in the conventional location. Production finally ceased when all existing stocks of chassis had been used.

Below:
A Sentinel model 4/4DV 7-8tonner showing the position of the underfloor engine. This was the standard Sentinel design.

Above:
Two 7-8ton models having a 16ft wheelbase and a 22ft long platform. These show the redesigned cab which appeared on later models.

Below:
The 6/6DV six-wheeler for 12ton payloads. It is fitted with a four-cylinder engine and has a 21ft 10in platform length.

Shelvoke and Drewry 1923-1992

The firm was started in 1923 by Harry Shelvoke and J. S. Drewry, both ex-employees of Lacre, and its first production was a small forward-control vehicle with a 2ton payload and 20in-diameter wheels called the Freighter. The driver half stood literally in-between the transverse engine and on his right and left had handles similar to a tram controller, one of which steered the vehicle and the other effected the speed change and reverse. The gearbox was a semi-automatic unit, with three speeds in either direction! The vehicles were popular as they had a low floor height of only 1ft 11in and this made them eminently suitable for refuse collecting and local delivery work. From 1932 until 1939 the firm also produced the Latil Tractor under licence from the French firm.

In 1946 the W-type freighter appeared and this had conventional controls. It was again popular with municipal authorities and many of the chassis were fitted with a rear-loading tipping body which compressed the refuse by gravity in its barrel-shaped shell. From 1961 the Pakamatic rear loading body in which the refuse was compressed by a mechanical ram was built. The latest type (from 1970) is the Revopak in which the contents are compressed by a rotary action. In both cases unloading was accomplished by a normal tipping action and gravity. The vehicles are powered by a variety of engines including Ford, Leyland and Perkins.

In 1971 S&D became part of the Butterfield-Harvey Group and from 1973 has used Motor Panels cabs on some of its products. From 1975 it instigated the Special Purpose Vehicles division which produces 4x4 and 6x4 off-the-road vehicles such as drilling rigs, military vehicles, airport crash tenders and from 1976 fire appliances. Some of the latter are built in conjunction with Carmichael of Worcester, which has undertaken the bodywork. Engines which can be fitted include the Cummins V8, the Perkins V8 or the Rolls-Royce straight-eight.

In 1984 the company merged with the US manufacturer Dempster, and adopted the new trading name Shelvoke Dempster. In 1980 the company continued its design for refuse collecting vehicles with the model P, using an Ogle-designed cab (identical to the Dennis Delta vehicles). Shelvoke Dempster have also produced some fire appliances using the same cab design. Leyland, Perkins or Rolls-Royce engines are fitted according to customer requirements.

Unfortunately, the economic down turn at the end of the 1980s took its toll, and Shelvoke Dempster ceased production in 1992.

Right:
This W-type refuse collector was produced in 1947 and is typical of the Shelvoke and Drewry design of that time. It had a four-cylinder side-valve engine of 67bhp. The cab could seat six loaders plus the driver. The side loading body had an 18cu yd capacity.

Thornycroft 1896-1962

The origins of Thornycroft go back to 1864 when John Isaac Thornycroft began building steam-driven launches for river work. Later he turned his attentions to steam-driven road vehicles and in 1896 produced a steam van, but he kept his marine interests. Early experiments with petrol and paraffin engines kept Thornycroft to the forefront of engineering and its J-type lorries of World War 1 fame were continued for civilian use for many years. In the 1930s Thornycroft made vehicles from 2ton to 15ton and for a wide variety of uses, which were extremely popular with operators both large and small. It also produced some vehicles for specialised work.

The War Department ordered some 5,000 vehicles during the last war, including the 4x4 Nubian and later the 6x4 Amazon model.

In 1948 the range was the Nippy 3ton, Sturdy 5/6ton, Sturdy 8ton tractor, the Amazon 12ton six-wheeler and the Trusty 15ton eight-wheeler. In 1950 the 12ton Trident rigid vehicle was introduced and the Sturdy revamped and called the Sturdy Star; the word 'Star' was also applied to the Nippy model. Shortly after this a new pressed-steel cab was introduced to the smaller vehicles in the range and this cab was shared with Guy Motors, although the two firms were not connected in any way.

The Nippy Star was replaced by the Swift and the Sturdy Star by the Swiftsure in 1957 when the Mastiff four-wheeled rigid seven-tonner appeared. In 1959/60 a new attractive cab with pronounced rounded corner panels was put on the market, but before they had become too familiar, Transport Equipment (Thornycroft) Ltd — to give the company its full title — was taken over by AEC and the range was trimmed down to the Nubian model and some special purpose vehicles. Eight years later the Basingstoke works were sold and all production transferred to Scammell at Watford.

Mention must be made of the Mighty Antar and Big Ben tractor units which were produced for special purpose and the haulage of indivisible loads. The former was designed for oil-field work but was also used by heavy haulage operators for gross weights in excess of 100ton. The latter vehicle appeared in 1954 as a six-wheel tractor for large loads of up to a maximum gross weight of 40ton using a new 11.33litre oil engine developing 155bhp from its six cylinders.

Below:
A 1950 3ton Nippy lorry, one of many supplied to British Railways. The former Great Western Railway operated a great number of Nippy 3ton vans.

Top:
A 1954 Trusty 8x4 platform lorry for 15ton payload. The girder is 48ft long and weighs 13ton.

Above:
The Trusty could also be purchased as a 4x2 tractor as shown here with a 3,200gal four compartment tanker trailer in 1955.

Above:
A Trident 9cu yd tipper on an 11ft 6in chassis. Body dimensions were 11ft 6in long by 7ft wide by 3ft high. Note the almost identical cab to those fitted to certain Guy vehicles.

Below:
The Swiftsure 1959 model which had an improved cab and external appearance. It had a 6-7ton payload capacity.

Top:
Designed originally for export to oil field operators etc, this Mighty Antar is proceeding through Edmonton (North London) in 1950. A smaller version of the Antar was introduced in the late 1950s named the Big Ben which had similar external appearance.

Above:
One of the last heavy goods designs to come out of the Basingstoke works before the company was acquired by AEC. This is a 1958 version of the Trusty eight-wheeler.

Trojan 1924-1962

Originally designed by L. H. Hounsfield and built by Leyland at its Kingston Works from 1924, the Trojan has chassisless construction, chain drive, solid tyres and a 10hp two-stroke engine, The first model had a carrying capacity of only 5cwt, but this was later uprated to 7cwt. Trojan manufactured vehicles itself at its Purley works from 1928 and a 10cwt version, basically similar to the 7cwt model appeared in 1930 which remained in production until 1942. In 1937 a more advance design was produced. The vehicles were popular with local tradesmen, but were extensively used by the Brooke Bond Tea Company.

In 1947 a completely new 15cwt van was put on the market, still with a two-stroke engine but an alternative Perkins P3V was also offered. This model continued in production until the company ceased to manufacture in 1959. The last design appeared in 1958 and was a forward-control 25cwt model again using the Perkins diesel engine. It was not an outstanding success in the popularity poll, although some were fitted with minibus bodies.

Below:
A Trojan series 7 one-ton van of 1957. It has a neat appearance with a wheelbase of 7ft 10in and an overall length of 13ft 11in. The Perkins P3V diesel engine developed 34bhp from its three cylinders and the vehicle was claimed to return 40mpg.

Vulcan 1903-1953

Reference to the dates in the heading of this chapter make this entry eligible. Vulcan was formed in 1903 to produce commercial vehicles and buses, which it did with varying success, but never reached the top of the league. The firm merged with Tilling Stevens in 1931 and production was transferred to Maidstone where it continued, although few buses were ever manufactured and only a handful of coaches which were on a modified goods chassis. In 1953 Tilling Stevens was taken over by the Rootes Group, which already had Commer and Karrier vehicles, and it was decided that Vulcan would be absorbed into those companies. Thus the name disappeared. The range at that time consisted of a forward-control 6ton vehicle usually fitted with a Perkins P6 diesel engine.

Right:
Intended for unveiling at the 1939 Commercial Motor Show, this 6ton Vulcan platform lorry was available in 1941 under Ministry of Transport licence. Powered by a four-cylinder engine of 78bhp it was the standard production model until Vulcan manufacture ceased; there was however a more modern cab on some later models.

Top:
The six-tonner has a 13ft wheelbase and 16ft body length. The dray illustrated is for the transport of crates of beers and mineral waters.

Fire Appliances

Up to the mid-1930s the old type fire appliance with the crew standing in the open holding on to the side of the escape, or sitting on bench type seats reminiscent of the old horse bus 'knifeboard' seating, was commonplace. Then to give the firemen some protection from the elements and some degree of comfort, the enclosed or limousine type bodywork was adopted.

During the war Auxiliary Fire Service (AFS) used many hundreds of Austin K2 chassis with an open-backed van body, extending ladders on the roof and towing a trailer pump. Such units did valiant work during the blitz in all parts of the country. After the war the Home Office specified some Bedford S-type chassis for emergency work and these become known as the Green Goddess type. They carried a pump capable of delivering 1,000gal of water per minute and a 35ft extending ladder on the roof. They were called out during the firemen's strike in 1979/80.

Up to the 1950s the main manufacturer of chassis for fire appliances was Dennis and

Leyland, later joined by AEC. In the 1970s, the main makers were again Dennis partnered by ERF plus Ford and Dodge, but in the 1980s fashion swung again to Dennis, Ford and Shelvoke.

Visible warning was given by up to four blue flashing lights adopted from 1961 and the bell has been superseded by the two-tone horn as an audible warning. Colour schemes have also

Below:

A typical example of a postwar fire appliance of 1949. The Dennis dual purpose vehicle was built to the specification of the Central Fire Brigades Advisory Committee and the Home Office. It was powered by a Rolls-Royce eight-cylinder 150bhp petrol engine giving the appliance a maximum speed of 60mph and acceleration from 0 to 40 in 30sec. The laden weight was 8ton and overall length 27ft 6in with a wheelbase of 13ft 6in. It carried a 100gal water tank for the ¾in rubber first aid hose which pumped at 25gal/min.

Above:
An ERF chassis fitted with Metz turntable ladder for Hampshire Fire Brigade.

changed, for the traditional red has given way to experiments in yellow, red and white, and it seems the latest is 'dayglo' red with polished aluminium panels and fittings for the lockers on the vehicle side.

The modern appliance — which has to conform to Home Office specifications — carries much more equipment than its predecessors of a couple of decades ago. With the advent of greater use of road transport which now carries chemicals, dangerous and inflammable liquids in bulk, and generally a greater risk of a major calamity, the Fire Brigade has to be ready to tackle many incidents which many not be actual fires. Again the modern forms of furniture and decorations can mean that if there is a fire poisonous smoke and fumes may have to be combatted, therefore breathing apparatus for all the crew has to be carried, along with foam making equipment and a host of other specialised gear to cope with the differing contingencies.

The term fire appliance — it should never be called an 'engine' — is used in the general sense and envelops many differing types of specialised vehicles — pump/escapes, turntable ladders, emergency tenders, hose-laying lorries, mobile control rooms and salvage corp tenders.

In addition to the normal appliances on the roads there are specialised vehicles which have been developed for airport and airfield services, but being off-the-road vehicles are beyond the scope of this book.

Above:
A Bedford general purpose appliance supplied to the Fife Fire Brigade in 1958. The whole of the front, cab roof, engine cowling and panel is polyester resin. The body was built by HCB (Hampshire Car Bodies).

Above:
ERF constructed the bodywork on the Dodge K850 chassis for the West Riding Fire Brigade appliance based at Wakefield.

Above:
An AEC Marquis fire appliance which is typical of a style built in the late 1950s. This was supplied to Leicester, but many were supplied to other Brigades including London. It is similar to the Dinky Toy model.

Below:
A Ford D13417 chassis with Cheshire Fire Engineering body for this water tender/ladder appliance supplied to Shropshire Fire Service in 1980. The chassis is not standard, but developed for the purpose by Ford's special vehicle engineering department and meets Home Office specification. It is powered by a Perkins 8.8litre V8 diesel producing 168bhp. The appliance carries 400gal of water, a 35ft two-section ladder and crew of six. Its gross laden weight is 11ton.

Above:
The Dennis R series of which there are many variants. This is a 1977 product.

Centre left:
Introduced in 1978 and used by many authorities including Surrey and Middlesex is this Shelvoke 4x2 chassis fitted with the four-door crew cab especially designed for fire use. The rest of the body and equipment was supplied by Cheshire Fire Engineering Ltd.

Bottom left:
The Land Rover was one of the smallest fire appliances. The 2litre engine drives the 150.200gal/min pump, and also supplied the first-aid reel from the 40gal tank mounted amidship. The all-up weight was 2ton.

Municipal Vehicles

Having devoted a short chapter to fire appliances, it is only right that a selection of ambulances and refuse collecting vehicles also be shown. While not so glamorous they also play their part for the community.

Changes have obviously been made in the period covered by this book, and as far as ambulances are concerned they have become more specialised, with plastics playing an important part in the interior fittings. Refuse collecting vehicles have become more hygienic and the days of the side-loaders with all the dust and dirt flying on the breeze have virtually disappeared.

Right:
A 1980 Ford Transit with Wadham Stringer body. A Ford SVO 3litre V6 petrol engine is fitted.

Below right:
The Karrier 1½ton chassis (now Dodge) from the Walk-thru van is fitted with a Dennis Ambulance body and is popular with many authorities having a top speed of about 60mph from the six-cylinder petrol engine of 2.96litre capacity which develops 85bhp.

Below:
A Lever-bodied Bedford in 1952 and now looking quite dated.

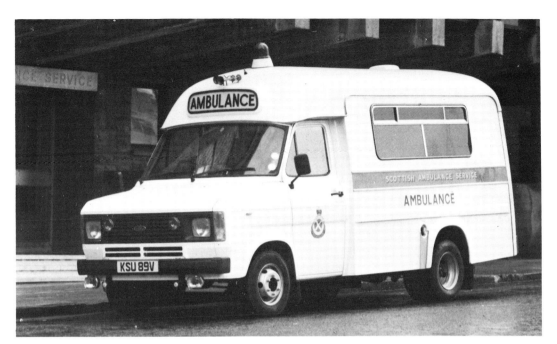

Top:
**The Morris FG series with wheelbase of
10ft 9in has a body by Wadham Stringer. This
model dates from 1963.**

Above:
**A Range Rover with ambulance body is used by
several hospitals and private institutions.**

Above:

A typical example of a small side-loading refuse collector of 1952. This Karrier Bantam had a capacity of 7cu yd.

Below:

In marked contrast to the above is this 1976 Karrier 8ton 13ft 6in wheelbase chassis with Glover, Webb & Liversidge continuous loading refuse collection body.

Above:
A Leyland Boxer chassis with Perkins engine and Jack Allen Colectomatic refuse collection body as supplied to the London Borough of Lambeth in 1981.

Right:
A Ford D500 with Eagle 800gal gully and cesspool emptier.

Breakdown Vehicles

The style and operation of breakdown vehicles has changed considerably over the years. The modern commercial and passenger vehicle has become more reliable, but mechanical troubles can never be ruled out and unfortunately there is always the problem of accidents, which with the coming of the motorways can be more serious when they happen. As legislation has permitted larger and heavier commercial vehicles on the roads, so the breakdown unit has had to follow suit. Nowadays it is a specialised vehicle, with — it is hoped — a specialised crew. The days of the simple rear mounted crane, often on an old lorry chassis, have gone except in the cases for the towing of private cars or light vans.

For a couple of decades after the last war, many operators of breakdown cranes used vehicles purchased from ex-WD sales, and a selection of ex-service vehicles could be seen operating in a civilian organisation but they have now almost disappeared from the scene. Many operators of such vehicles were ex-servicemen who were starting out in business, some with improvised home-made equipment. It was also the time of the birth of the 'accident pirates', and these small firms and individuals would position their vehicle in a strategic position alongside a main arterial road, listening to police traffic messages on short-wave radio. They often arrived at the scene of an accident before the emergency services! the 'pirates' usually had small vehicles, little equipment, and often even less knowledge of lifting and recovering a vehicle from a difficult position.

It was not so long ago that the only really heavy recovery vehicle belonged to the County Fire Brigade or some of the larger municipal transport undertakings, or one of the specialist transport contractors such as Pickfords, although the latter usually only dealt with its own vehicles, unless in an emergency they received a police request for assistance.

The modern heavy recovery vehicle is usually fitted with four-wheel drive, large power-operated winches, twin-boom cranes (developed from an American idea), heavy-duty hydraulic jacks, oxy-acetylene cutting apparatus and a host of other equipment. A recent innovation is a large inflatable air-cushion for lifting and to absorb the impact and minimise further damage when righting an overturned vehicle.

Below:
An ex-American Diamond Tank Transporter unit working as a civilian recovery vehicle. The Hercules diesel engine still powered the unit which could tow up to 50ton. Maximum lift was 12ton and maximum on winch pull 17ton, increased by 10 or even 20 times by the use of pulley blocks.

Above:

The modern recovery vehicle is exemplified by this 1978 Ford 4x2 Transcontinental fitted with powerful equipment and lifting and winching facilities.

Below:

For smaller jobs and private cars the Ford Transit is ideal and this version is fitted with a Holmes Cadet 1000 crane. The Cadet is available with electrical winching or with a lift chain and boom end, and features an electro-hydraulic boom lift for easy manoeuvrability.

Battery Electrics

By reason of carrying its own power supply in the form of a large bank of batteries, such vehicles have remained in the light van class. In demand prewar and, of course, during the war when petrol was rationed, their popularity declined except for milk rounds. Their limited range and low speeds have restricted them to local delivery work.

However with recent developments in battery technology and electric motors which use less current, and spurred on by the anti-pollution campaigners there has been an increase in experimental activity. Ford Transits have been converted and have been tried by the Post Office, while the North Western Electricity Board even has a battery driven Leyland Boxer van. An experimental taxi and even a full-size single-deck bus towing a trailer containing the batteries have been in use. Now the Bedford CF, Leyland Sherpa and Dodge 50-series vans are all available in battery-electric form, but a high purchase price, limited range and reduced payload have conspired against large-scale production.

It is possible that in another two decades, the battery electric vehicle may prove more feasible and commonplace.

Below:
A Smiths NCB one-ton van for British Rail. It has a range of 37 miles and a maximum speed of 18mph fully laden on a level road.

Above:
A one-ton Morrison Electricar of 1954.

Left:
The ubiquitous milk float. This one is a Wales & Edwards 25cwt long wheelbase chassis supplied in 1958 with a speed of 12-14mph.

Above:
A modern battery electric vehicle in use by the Post Office, supplied by Crompton Electric Vehicles.

Left:
The latest concept in battery electric vehicles. A Bedford CF van/minibus in experimental use for local service. Several experimental vehicles are being so designed with good performance being acclaimed.

283

Fairground Vehicles

Road transport is the life-blood of the travelling showman, whose transport is usually varied and interesting. As the actual mileage covered in a year is small by comparison with a haulage business, showmen inevitably purchase their transport vehicles secondhand from recognised haulage contractors or operators and this is where many fine vehicles end their days, long after their compatriots have left the general road haulage field.

Many of the vehicles are rebodied to suit the specialised loads they will be conveying; often the body is taken from a previous vehicle, and there are still a few examples of wooden-planked van-type bodies in existence — the body sometimes being three times the age of the chassis it is upon. The modifications made are often ingenious and demonstrate the competence of the showman as a mechanical engineer.

By the very nature of the loads carried the most popular vehicle is the diesel powered prime mover or tractive unit which can carry a generating set where the articulated coupling gear was placed and can also haul up to three large trailers, each carrying a maximum load. a large 'ride' such as as Dodgem set usually requires at lease two rigid eight-wheelers each pulling a massive trailer, plus the prime mover (with generating equipment) pulling two trailers — often the pay box and control desk plus the operator's own living wagon (or caravan).

Until recently articulated semi-trailer units were not favoured by showmen because of the difficulty of manoeuvring especially over rough terrain and their inability to pull another trailer. However, over the past 10 years of so, new rides and machines have been designed and built for their base or platform to be permanently fixed to a semi-trailer. Such rides as lifting paratroopers, satellites and their associated meteorites, hurricane jets etc are arranged to fold up to the sides of the main unit on the semi-trailer to make a compact although unwieldy looking load which is then coupled direct to the tractive unit via the normal fifth wheel.

Current vehicle legislation has made it prudent (and sometimes necessary!) for the showmen to have more up-to-date vehicles than hitherto, thus many of the real antiques such as the Tilling Stevens, ex-WD vehicles etc have virtually disappeared, but the fairground can still have some interesting and unique examples of specialised transport.

Below:
This 1944 Leyland van was originally owned by Callard & Bowser and now with a Showman. Seen at Wanstead Flats in 1981. *VRPL*

Top right:
The ex-Army AEC Matador 4x4 gun tractor is becoming quite rare on the fairground nowadays. This one was owned by Biddalls and is seen in 1965. *VRPL*

Centre right:
A little bit of glamour on the scene! Exquisite signwriting on Bob Wilson's Atkinson van at Ealing in 1967. *VRPL*

Below:
A home-built body on this eight-wheeler with distinctive lettering. Note the colossal overhang at the rear of the van. *VRPL*

Top left:
A Scammell design of 1946 especially for the Showman — the Showtrac. The engine is a Gardner 6LW developing 102bhp. The gross train weight is 45ton and the diesel engine inside the body at the rear drives a generator with a maximum output of 450A. There is also a winch and a ballast block for adhesion. *VRPL*

Bottom left:
A veteran AEC Mammoth Major eight-wheeled van in use by Forrests Amusements photographed on Blackheath in April 1973. *VRPL*

Top right:
A sign of the times! A Foden articulated unit with Henry Smith's complete and self-contained Flying Orbiter load. The semi-trailer forms the base of the machine when in use. Note the paybox in the centre. Seen at Newhaven in August 1978. *VRPL*

Centre right:
Two dignified stalwarts of the fairground! Edwards's of Swindon with two Scammell tractors *The Lady Margaret* and *The Churchill*. Edwards names nearly all of its vehicles which are always immaculately turned out, lined and lettered. Note the levelling block of wood under one of the front wheels. Seen at Hampstead Heath in 1974. *VRPL*

Bottom right:
A veteran Atkinson eight-wheeled van in use by John Biddall of London at Hampstead Heath. *VRPL*

Above:
Living accommodation for fairground workers is provided by this ERF van with dormitory accommodation at the rear. It belongs to London Showman Fred Gray and seen in 1968 on Wimbledon Common. *VRPL*

Below:
Another Scammell tractor of the type favoured by the petrol companies and now in fairground use. This nicely lettered version is owned by Armstrongs and about to reverse with a box trailer to pull it into position. Wanstead Flats in 1979. *VRPL*